QuarkXPress Power Shortcuts

David Blatner

Peachpit Press

QuarkXPress Power Shortcuts

by David Blatner

Peachpit Press
1249 Eighth Street
Berkeley, CA 94710
510/524-2178
800/283-9444
510/524-2221 (fax)

Find us on the World Wide Web at: http://www.peachpit.com

To report errors, please send a note to errata@peachpit.com

Peachpit Press is a division of Pearson Education

Copyright ©2002 by David Blatner

Acquisitions Editor: Beth Millett
Development Editor: Susan Hobbs
Managing Editor: Thomas F. Hayes
Project Editors: Tricia Liebig, Karen S. Shields
Indexer: Tina Trettin
Proofreader: Plan-in Publishing
Team Coordinator: Sharry Lee Gregory
Interior Designer: Anne Jones
Cover Designer: Maureen Forys
Page Layout: Gloria Schurick

ISBN 0-7897-2433-2
Library of Congress Catalog Card Number 00-103417
9 8 7 6 5 4 3 2 1

Printed and bound in the United States of America

About the Author

David Blatner is arguably the world's most-recognized authority on QuarkXPress, and the author or co-author of a number of books, including the award-winning bestseller *Real World QuarkXPress 5* (formerly *The QuarkXPress 4 Book*), *Real World Photoshop 6*, *Real World Scanning and Halftones*, *Real World InDesign 2*, *Judaism For Dummies*, and *The Joy of Pi*. David has presented at conferences around North America, South Africa, and Japan, including Macworld, Seybold Seminars, and The Photoshop Conference. You can find him at www.moo.com.

Dedication

To my friend and colleague Stephen F. Roth, who first said, "Hey, have you ever thought of writing a book?"

Acknowledgments

In this world of desktop publishing, you'd think that a guy could sit down and take credit for producing a book all by himself. But the truth is that this never happens. Sure, my name is on the cover, but heaps of work were done by Beth Millett and Suz Hobbs at Que Publishing, as well as my technical editor, Richard Romano. Myke Ninness was an inspiration, and Don Munsil was indirectly involved by encouraging me to always figure out the most efficient way to do anything in life (to the point of neurosis, probably). My office-mates over the past few years—Glenn Fleishman, Jeff Carlson, Jeff Tolbert, Steve Roth, Ole Kvern, Toby Malina, Agen Schmitz, and Brett Baker—are too awesome for words, and my wife and partner Debbie Carlson is the most wonderful support a guy could have. Thank you all!

Hey, XPress Yourself!

As the reader of this book, you're my most important critic and commentator. I value your opinion and want to know what I'm doing right, what I could do better, what your favorite tips and tricks are, and any other words of wisdom you're willing to pass my way.

Please note that while I can occasionally help you with technical problems, due to the high volume of mail I receive, it sometimes takes me weeks to get back to you. In general, if you need technical support, it's best to contact Quark's tech support department directly at (303) 894-8899 or on the Web at http://www.quark.com/support/.

Also, if you enjoy this book, take a look at two of my other books: *Real World QuarkXPress* and *Real World Photoshop*.

E-mail:	qxbook@moo.com
Web site:	http://www.peachpit.com/blatner/
Mail:	David Blatner, moo.com
	c/o Peachpit Press
	1249 Eighth Street
	Berkeley, CA 94710

Contents

Contents

Menus

Contents

Contents

Pictures and Lines   107

Introduction

In this fast-paced, high-charged, hyper-productive world, it pays to be efficient. (Actually, if you work by the hour, it doesn't. If you're one of the many workers who are still paid hourly, you might as well just stop reading this now—this book is about efficiency, not how to stretch out your work for the extra bucks. On the other hand, your client or boss never need know that you've gotten more efficient!)

As I was saying, it pays to be efficient, and there are many ways to become efficient. The problem is that most people focus on increasing productivity by buying a new computer, or more RAM, or a video acceleration card. Unfortunately, the best way to become efficient isn't anywhere near as sexy as buying any of these toys. The best way to become efficient is not to speed up your system, but rather to speed up *you*. And after more than 14 years working with QuarkXPress, I've found that the best way to speed up *you* is to learn keyboard shortcuts.

Let's face it: Learning a keyboard shortcut ain't fun. If, however, you take the time to learn the shortcuts now, you're more than repaid with fun later. It's fun to show off in front of your boss. Most of all, it's fun to get your work done faster so that you can surf the 'net while your colleagues (who don't own this book) are still using menus and pushing a mouse all over their screens.

Don't get me wrong. I like menus and mice and all the trappings of a graphic user interface. But I've used computers long enough to know that DOS and CPM and Unix will always be more efficient when you're keeping your hands on the keyboard. Keyboard shortcuts give you the best of both worlds—keeping your hands on the keyboard in a graphic user interface.

Using This Book

There are a number of ways to use this book (none of them includes reading it from cover to cover). My suggestion is to plop it down next to your computer, and every time you reach for a menu item, force yourself to stop, pick up the book, and look up the equivalent keyboard shortcut. Sure, this slows you down in the short term, but after looking up a keyboard shortcut three times, your brain will get so tired of looking it up that the shortcut will stick. (This is a well-known neurological function, which scientists call *Keybordus cranial embeddus*.)

By the way, if you're still using QuarkXPress 4, don't worry. Quark changed very few keyboard shortcuts between versions 4 and 5, and the few that are specific to version 5 are marked clearly with the QX5 icon.

Windows Versus Macintosh

Hey, do you know the difference between the Option key on the Macintosh and the Alt key on a Windows system? Someone labeled them differently. That's it. The same thing goes for the Command (Cmd) key on the Mac (sometimes known as the Apple key or the Cloverleaf key) and the Control (Ctrl) key in Windows. People get so bent out of shape with their *Mac versus Windows* religious wars, but there are more similarities than you might think.

Nonetheless, in this book, I've clearly stated both the Macintosh and the Windows shortcuts next to each other because I don't want someone to throw a brick through my office window for being biased.

Of course, the Mac has a Control key, too. In 98 percent of the cases, Control on the Mac is the equivalent of pressing the right mouse button in Windows. That wasn't so hard, was it?

Get a Macro Program

There's no keyboard shortcut in QuarkXPress for Collect for Output (found under the File menu). Does that annoy you? It should. It means every time you use that feature, you have to use the menu. Fortunately, you can buy a utility program that enables you to build macros, like CE Software's QuicKeys (available on Macintosh and Windows; see www.cesoft.com) or OneClick (Mac only; see www.westcodesoft.com). A macro lets you assign any keyboard shortcut to any menu item, or even a sequence of actions you might perform frequently. In my opinion, they shouldn't even sell Macs or PCs without a copy of QuicKeys preinstalled. It's that important to an efficient workflow.

First Steps in Cutting Corners

No one in their right mind knows *all* the keyboard shortcuts in a program. (That pretty clearly says something about me, doesn't it?) There are over 400 shortcuts listed in this book. If you try to memorize them all at once, the friction in your brain will cause you to spontaneously combust. Instead, start with just a few important shortcuts, and work your way up from there as necessary.

Note that in some cases, there is more than one way to perform the same task in QuarkXPress. It's worth learning them all for maximum efficiency. That way, if both hands are on the keyboard you can do one thing, if one hand is on the keyboard and one is on the mouse, you can do something else, and so on.

Here's a list of a few of my favorite keyboard shortcuts and shortcut techniques. Master these and you'll be well on your way to QuarkXPress Efficiency Nirvana.

Don't Panic!

I once had a guy in one of my seminars who asked me what the trick was when building complex shapes with the Polygon tool in XPress. (Quark has since replaced this tool with the Bézier tool.) His problem, he explained, was that he sometimes couldn't find the first point in the polygon and so he could never close the shape and switch to a different tool. I asked him what he usually did when he got stuck in this position. His response: "Reboot the machine."

Look—the most important lesson you can learn about QuarkXPress is *Don't Panic*. If you think you've gotten yourself stuck in some uncomfortable position in XPress, take a deep breath and remember two basic keyboard shortcuts. First, Cmd+Period (Mac) or the Esc key (Windows) cancels whatever you're working on. Second, Cmd+Z (Mac) or Ctrl+Z (Windows) is the Undo feature.

If you've messed up the shape of a box accidentally, you can Cmd+Z/Ctrl+Z it. If you type 45 degrees in the Rotation field of the Measurements palette and XPress tells you that you can't do this because rotating the box this much would put it off the paste-board, don't panic. Instead just press Cmd+period or Esc. If you're drawing with the Bézier text box tool and you can't find the first point (to close the box), just pick a different tool in the Tool palette—preferably with a keyboard shortcut. (See the "Picking Tools" section later in this introduction.) It's never so bad that you have to panic.

Navigating Dialog Boxes

We'll be looking at a number of ways to open dialog boxes in XPress, but once they're open, what do you do? Remember that you can always press Tab to jump from one field in the dialog box to the next, and you can Shift+Tab to move backward from field to field. Once you get to know the various dialog boxes better, you'll remember exactly how many tabs you need to get to the field you want to edit.

Similarly, you can Cmd+Tab (Macintosh) or Ctrl+Tab (Windows) from one tab to another within a tabbed dialog box. (See the caveat to this "Picking Tools" section later in this introduction.)

Once you're done in a dialog box, press Enter or Return instead of clicking the OK button, or Cmd+period (Mac) or Esc (Windows) to press the Cancel button. Granted, these hardly seem like important tips, but these are the sorts of actions you perform dozens or even hundreds of times each day. Becoming a little more efficient saves time in the long run.

Picking Tools

There's no keyboard shortcut for selecting a specific tool in the Tool palette. Period. However, you can select the *next* or *previous* tool in the palette with a keystroke. On the Macintosh, press Cmd+Tab to select the next tool and Cmd+Shift+Tab to select the previous tool. In Windows, press Ctrl+Alt+Tab and Ctrl+Shift+Alt+Tab.

Unfortunately, in Mac OS 8, 9, and 10 (OS X), Apple confiscated the Cmd+Tab and Cmd+Shift+Tab keyboard shortcuts for their own use. Now these shortcuts switch from one running application to another. Unfortunately, that means you cannot use these important shortcuts in XPress anymore. Instead, you can move up and down the Tool palette by adding either the Ctrl or Option keys, such as Cmd+Option+Tab, and Cmd+Option+Shift+Tab.

In OS 8 or 9, you can also use the Mac OS Help system to change the Application Switcher's keystroke:

1. Go to the Finder and select Help Center in the Help menu.

2. Type **application switcher** into the Find field and then click Search.

3. You should see an item called **Switching Between Open Programs**. Click on this item.

4. Toward the end of the description, you should see a link to **Help me modify the keyboard shortcuts**. Click this and follow the instructions to change the keystroke. If the script asks you to find the Application Switcher, it's hiding in the Extensions folder, inside the System Folder.

Moving Through Measurements

The Measurements palette is central control for your documents, so the faster you can move through it, the better. Cmd+Option+M (Mac) and Ctrl+Alt+M (Windows) jumps to the first field of this palette. From there, you can Tab forward or Shift+Tab backward through the palette's fields, just like the fields in dialog boxes.

My favorite trick, however, is to add the Shift key to this keystroke—Cmd+Option+Shift+M or Ctrl+Alt+Shift+M— which jumps directly to the Font field in the Measurements palette. From there, you can just start typing the name of a font. For instance, if you want to change some text to Palatino, hit this keystroke and then type **P**. QuarkXPress picks the first **P** font you have, which is probably Palatino. If you needed **Perpetua** instead, you'd probably have to type **Pe**. You only have to type as much of the font name as XPress needs to guess the font correctly.

Use the Built-in Math

Do you need to cut the width of a box in half? What about move a box over 2.375 inches? Don't reach for your calculator— QuarkXPress has one built in! You can perform math in every palette and dialog box in QuarkXPress, a fact that can save you an incredible amount of time and frustration.

To cut the width of a box in half, place the cursor after the value in the Width field (W:) field in the Measurements palette and type /2. The slash character means divide. Similarly, you could do the same thing by typing *.5 (which means to multiply by one-half). To move a box to the right, use the + character in the X-origin field of the Measurements palette; to move it to the left, use the - (hyphen) character.

Note that you can mix and match measurement systems, so even if a palette or dialog box is displaying inches, you can type in picas or centimeters or whatever. However, if you want to use a different measurement system, you have to include "p" for picas, "mm" for millimeters, the double-straight quotes for inches, and so on.

Grab the Grabber Hand

If you're still using the scroll bars to the right or bottom of your document window, there's no way you're really being efficient with QuarkXPress. Instead, use the Grabber Hand, which you can get either from the Tool palette (the slow way) or by holding down the Option (Mac) or Alt (Windows) key. Just hold down the modifier key; then click anywhere on the page and drag. This is definitely the fastest way to navigate around your page.

Of course, the Grabber Hand isn't much help if you need to move across multiple pages. In that case, you want to press Shift+Page Down to move to the next page or Shift+Page Up to jump to the previous page.

The "Direct Select" Tool

Need to move a box when you have the Content tool selected? No problem. Just hold down the Cmd key (Mac) or Ctrl key (Windows). This switches the cursor to the Item tool temporarily (until you let go of the modifier key).

Even better, this Temporary Item tool acts as a direct-select tool. If you have a group of objects selected, you can move a single item in the group with this keystroke. Also—here's one I use all the time—double-clicking on an object with the Item tool opens the Modify dialog box; or, if you have any other tool selected, Cmd+double-click (Mac) or Ctrl+double-click (Windows) does the same.

Make Style Sheets Fast

The fastest way to make a style sheet is to format some text, place the cursor in it, and use the context-sensitive menu in the Style Sheets palette. Most people just stare blankly at me when I say this, or they insist that there are no context-sensitive menus in QuarkXPress. They're wrong. If you hold down the Ctrl key (on Macintosh) or the right mouse button (in Windows) and then click on any of the style sheet names in the Style Sheets palette (a text box has to be selected for this to work), XPress offers you a little pop-up menu with the option to create a new style sheet, or edit, delete, or duplicate the style sheet you clicked on. If you select New, all you have to do is type in a name for your style sheet and then click OK. The style sheet is created with all the formatting of the text you formatted.

Managing Pictures

Every now and again, someone loses a picture in a picture box. They don't delete it; instead, they simply move it outside the boundaries of the box so they can't see it anymore. Eeeek! Don't worry. All you have to do is press Cmd+Shift+M (Mac) or Ctrl+Shift+M (Windows). This automatically centers the picture in the picture box.

Need to scale the picture to fit the box? No problem. Cmd+Shift+F (Mac) or Ctrl+Shift+F (Windows) stretches the picture to fit the box. Unfortunately, it does this disproportionately. Better to add the Option or Alt key to this lineup, which stretches the picture but maintains its proportions.

In XPress 5, you can even make the picture box fit the picture by selecting Fit Box to Picture from the context-sensitive menu (Ctrl+click or Right-button-click on the picture).

Patience Is a Virtue

When you click and drag a picture with the Item tool, all you see while dragging is a gray outline of the box. Same thing goes with a text box. And you get the same result when cropping, scaling, or rotating a box. However, I don't find a gray box particularly interesting to look at. Instead, try holding down the mouse button for about one second after clicking before dragging. Here is one place where patience is a virtue—by waiting a moment before dragging, XPress actually shows you the text or picture box as you crop, scale, rotate, or move it.

If you find this useful, you might consider changing the Delay field in the Application Preferences dialog box by using Cmd+Option+Shift+Y on the Mac, or Ctrl+Alt+Shift+Y in Windows. Set it down to .1, and you get this live refresh almost immediately.

Palettes

Tool Palette

Show/Hide Tool Palette

Menu: View→Show/Hide Tools

Both: F8

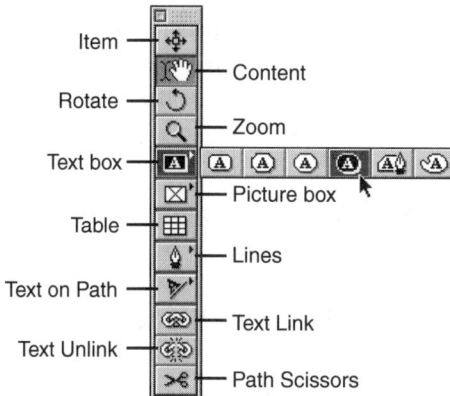

Palettes

Tool Palette Orientation

Windows: Ctrl+Alt+double-click on title bar

Some people like the Tool palette to be arranged horizontally instead of vertically. Unfortunately, there's no way to do this on the Macintosh.

Next Tool in Tool Palette

Mac: Cmd+Tab or Option+F8

Windows: Ctrl+Alt+Tab or Ctrl+F8

If Tool palette isn't showing, this keystroke acts like Show Tools.

Previous Tool in Tool Palette

Mac: Cmd+Shift+Tab or Option+Shift+F8

Windows: Ctrl+Alt+Shift+Tab or Ctrl+F8

See the caveat in the previous shortcut if you're on the Macintosh and this keyboard shortcut doesn't work anymore.

Keep a Tool Selected in Tool Palette

Mac: Option+click in Tool palette

Windows: Alt+click Tool

I find this sticky tool feature especially useful when trying to link a number of boxes together. If you don't use this keystroke, the Tool palette always reverts back to the Item or Content tool (whichever you used last).

Toggle Item/Content Tool in Tool Palette

Both: Shift+F8

To be honest, the only people who use this are people who play the piano and feel comfortable reaching an octave. For everyone else, the Next/Previous Tool keystrokes are usually easier to move back and forth between the two tools.

Tool Palette Preferences

Menu: Edit→Preferences→Document (version 4.x) or
Edit→Preferences (version 5); then choose Tools tab

Both: Double-click tool in Tool palette

The more you customize QuarkXPress to the way you work, the more efficient you'll be. Many people set the background color and runaround settings for text boxes to None every time they draw a box. Wouldn't it be easier just to change the preferences for the Text Box tool so that it always draws boxes with these settings? Just double-click on the Text Box tool and then click the Modify button to change its default settings.

Note that if a document is open when you change the tool preferences, the change is only made for that one document. If no documents are open, the tool changes for all documents you create from then on, but not previously built documents.

Click here to change how
the selected tools work.

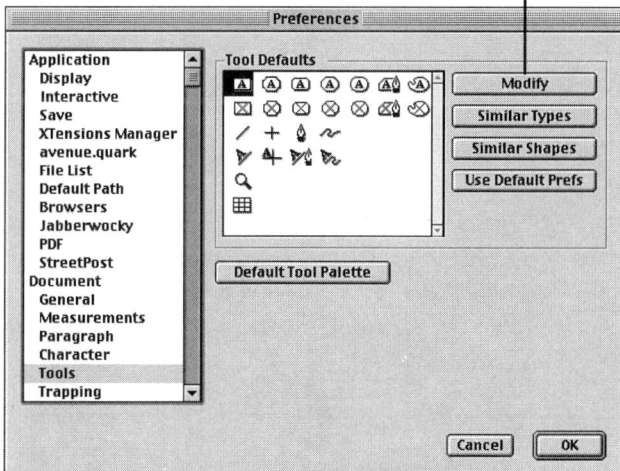

The Tool Preferences dialog
box in QuarkXPress 5

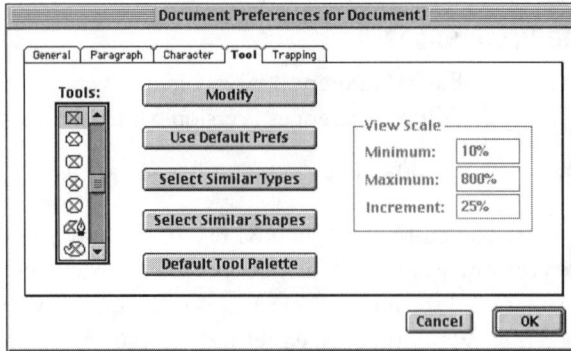

The Tool Preferences dialog
box in QuarkXPress 4

Measurements Palette

Show/Hide Measurements Palette

Menu: View→Show/Hide Measurements

Both: F9

When text box is selected

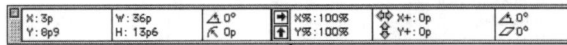

When picture box is selected

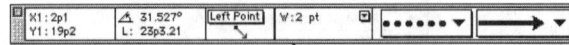

When line is selected

When Bézier line is selected

Go to Measurements Palette (First X Field)

Mac: Cmd+Option+M

Windows: Ctrl+Alt+M

This also opens the Measurements palette, if it is hidden. Once you're in the palette, you can Tab forward or Shift+Tab backward through the fields.

Jump to Font Field in Measurements Palette

Mac: Cmd+Option+Shift+M or Shift+F9

Windows: Ctrl+Alt+Shift+M or Shift+F9

This also opens the Measurements palette, if it is hidden. Remember that you don't have to type in the whole font name here. You can often get away with just typing one or two characters and XPress will guess the rest. Or, if you have 200 fonts loaded and you know the font you want starts with a J (but you can't remember exactly how to spell it), just type **J** and then click on the little arrow pop-up menu next to the Font field. Voilá! You're already in the J's!

Next Font in List (in Measurements Palette)

Mac: Option+F9

Windows: Ctrl+F9

The next font is chosen alphabetically by the bitmap suitcase font name, so if you're using Adobe Type Reunion or TypeTamer (www.typetamer.com)—or some other utility that unifies font families by name on the Macintosh—the change from one font to the next may seem random.

Previous Font in List (in Measurements Palette)

Mac: Option+Shift+F9

Windows: Ctrl+Shift+F9

The previous font in the list is chosen alphabetically by the bitmap suitcase font name, so if you're using Adobe Type Reunion—or some other utility that unifies font families by name on the Mac—the movement from the current font to the previous one may seem random.

Change Leading/Kerning/Tracking By Fine Increments

Mac: Option+click on the up, down, left, right arrow buttons

Windows: Alt+click on the buttons

When text is selected in a text box, clicking on the left and right arrow buttons in the Measurements palette typically adds or removes 10 units of kerning or tracking. The up and down arrow buttons add or remove 1 point of leading. Adding Option (Mac) or Alt (Windows) changes this to 1 unit of kerning and .1 point of leading. I much prefer to use the keyboard shortcuts for this kind of thing (see the shortcut "Increase Leading 1/10 Point" in Chapter 5, "Text").

Change Picture Offset By Fine Increments

Mac: Option+click on the up, down, left, right arrow buttons

Windows: Alt+click on the buttons

Clicking on the up, down, right, and left buttons in the Measurements palette (when a picture is selected) typically moves the picture in the box by 1 point (about .014 inch). Adding the Option (Mac) or Alt (Windows) key changes this to .1 point (about .001 inch). I much prefer to use the arrow keys instead. Option/Alt along with the Arrow keys performs the same magic.

Document Layout Palette

Show/Hide Document Layout Palette

Menu: View→Show/Hide Document Layout

Mac: F10

Windows: F4

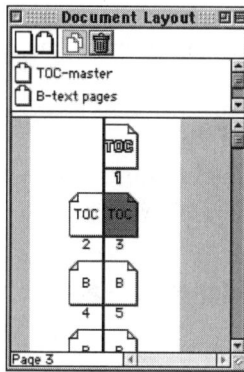

Open Section Dialog Box

Menu: Page→Section

Both: Select page in Document Layout palette; then click on the page field in the lower-left corner of the palette.

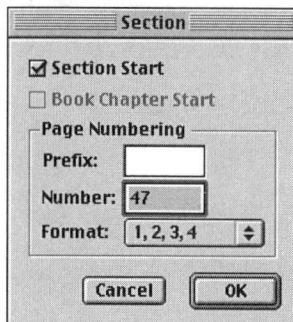

Palettes

Find Absolute Page Number

Mac: Option+click on the page in the Document Layout palette

Windows: Alt+click on the page in the Document Layout palette

The absolute page number represents the number of pages from the first page in the document. For instance, **+3** means **the third page of the document**. You can use this absolute value anywhere you need to type a page number, including the Print dialog box.

Display Page or Master Page

Both: Double-click on the page or master page icon in the Document Layout palette

Apply Master Page to Document Page

Mac: Select document page(s); then Option+click on master page icon

Windows: Select document page(s); then Alt+click on master page icon

Both: Drag the master page icon over the page. (This only works for one page at a time.)

Don't forget that you can select contiguous pages in the Document Layout palette by holding down the Shift key when you click. You can select discontiguous pages with the Cmd (Mac) or Ctrl (Windows) key.

Moving Pages

Menu: Page→Move

Mouse: Drag page(s)

When you drag one or more pages in the Document Layout palette, pay attention to the cursor icon. If it's a page outline, it means **put the page here**. A black arrow means **put the page(s) in the page flow starting here**. In most cases, you want the black arrow—unless you're creating a three-page spread.

Delete Page(s) or Master Page

Menu: Page→Delete

Mouse: Select page(s) and then click the Delete button

Add the Option (Mac) or Alt (Windows) key to delete without seeing the annoying **Are you sure you want to do this** alert.

Style Sheets Palette

Show/Hide Style Sheets Palette

Menu: View→Show/Hide Style Sheets

Both: F11

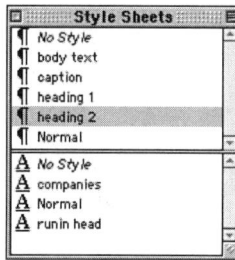

Context-Sensitive Menu in Style Sheets Palette

Mac: Ctrl+click in Style Sheets palette

Windows: Right-mouse-button click in Style Sheets palette

This only works when the Style Sheets palette is active; in other words, when a text box is selected with the Content tool.

Create New Style Sheet

Both: Manually format some text and then, with the cursor in that text, select New from the Context-sensitive menu. (See the previous shortcut.) Many people eschew style sheets because they think styles take too long to create. This shortcut certainly blows that myth out of the water.

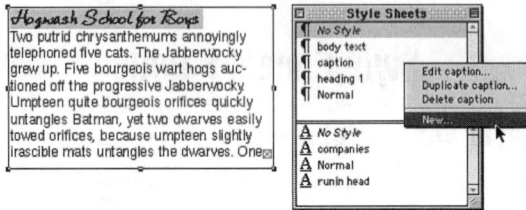

Apply Absolute Style Sheet

Mac: Option+click on style sheet name

Windows: Alt+click on style sheet name

This is the same thing as applying No Style and then applying the style sheet. It wipes out *all* local formatting in the paragraph—or, in the case of character style sheets, all local formatting in the selected text.

Edit Style Sheet

Menu: Edit→Style Sheets

Mac: Cmd+click in Style Sheets palette or Shift+F11

Windows: Ctrl+click in Style Sheets palette or Shift+F11

While Shift+F11 works at any time, Cmd+click or Ctrl+click only works when the Style Sheets palette is active; in other words, when a text box is selected with the Content tool.

Compare Style Sheets

Mac: Option+click on Append button

Windows: Alt+click on Append button

You can select two style sheets in the Edit Style Sheet dialog box by Cmd+clicking (Mac) or Ctrl+clicking (Windows) on each style sheet; then, when you hold down the Option/Alt key, the Append button turns into a Compare button. Press this button, and XPress shows you how the two styles are different by displaying the differences in bold.

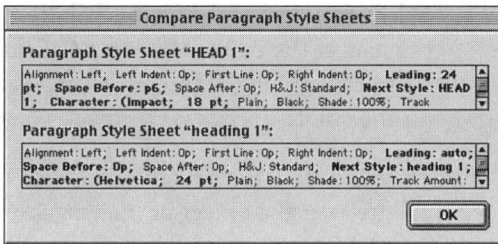

Colors Palette

Show/Hide Colors Palette

Menu: View→Show/Hide Colors

Both: F12

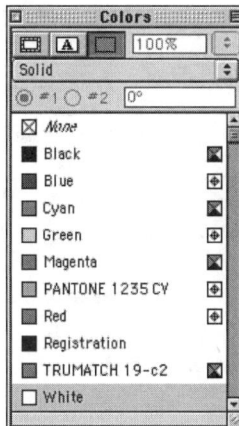

Palettes

Edit Color

Menu: Edit→Colors

Mac: Cmd+click in Colors palette

Windows: Ctrl+click in Colors palette

This only works when the Colors palette is active; in other words, when an object is selected.

Apply a Color

Both: Select the icon in the Colors palette that describes the part of the object you want to colorize—Line, Item, Background, Text, or Picture—and then click on the color.

Mouse: Drag-and-drop the swatch color from the Colors palette over the object or frame that you want to colorize.

If you want to apply a color to several objects on your page, drag the color's swatch from the Colors palette over the first object; then hold down the Cmd key (Mac) or Ctrl key (Windows) as you drag the swatch off the object and on top of the next object. When the Cmd/Ctrl key is held down, the color sticks to the object. Weird, but true.

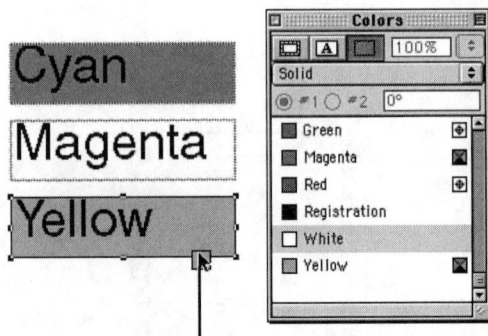

Cyan

Magenta

Yellow

Colors

100%

Solid

#1 #2 0°

Green
Magenta
Red
Registration
White
Yellow

Drop color swatch on
background or border
to apply color.

Index Palette

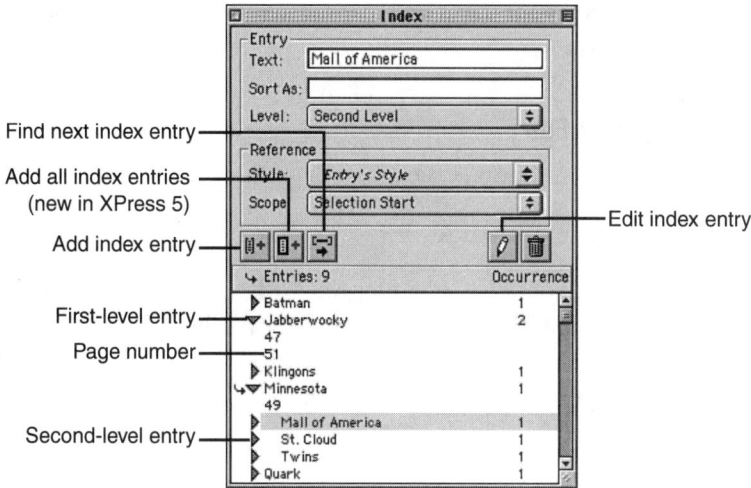

Find next index entry

Add all index entries (new in XPress 5)

Add index entry

Edit index entry

First-level entry

Page number

Second-level entry

Highlight Text Field in Index Palette

Mac: Cmd+Option+I

Windows: Ctrl+Alt+I

This is also the fastest way to open the Index palette, if it's hidden.

Add Text to Index

Mac: Cmd+Option+Shift+I

Windows: Ctrl+Alt+Shift+I

This automatically adds any selected text to your index using the last-used Level, Style, and Scope settings.

Edit Index Entry

Both: Double-click on index entry

If you double-click on the index entry name, you can edit how it appears in the index. If you double-click on the index entry's page number, QuarkXPress displays the index entry in the document window. If you don't see the page numbers, click on the gray tri-angle (Mac) or plus sign (Windows). This is a great way to navi-gate around your document! From there, you can edit that single index entry.

Find First Index Entry

Mac: Option+click

Windows: Alt+click

When you hold down the Option/Alt key, the Find Next Entry button in the Index palette changes to the Find First Entry; in other words, it searches from the beginning of the story instead of from the position of the text cursor.

Book Palette

Create New Book File

Menu: File→New→Book

You can make as many Book palettes as you want, but you shouldn't put the same document in two or more books. Also, note that you can put these book files on a server, and have multi-ple users open them at the same time; however, you shouldn't let Macintosh and Windows users access the book files at the same time—just one platform or the other.

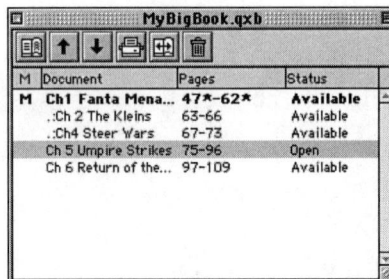

Palettes

Open Chapter

Both: Double-click on document

When working with documents in a Book palette, it's always best to open them from the Book palette itself. Otherwise, the palette can't tell that you have edited the files.

Change Chapter Order

Mac: Option+drag document name

Windows: Alt+drag document name

Mouse: Click the Up or Down buttons in palette

When you change the order of a document, XPress automatically updates all the page numbers.

Hyperlinks Palette

Open Hyperlinks Palette

Menu: View→Show/Hide Hyperlinks

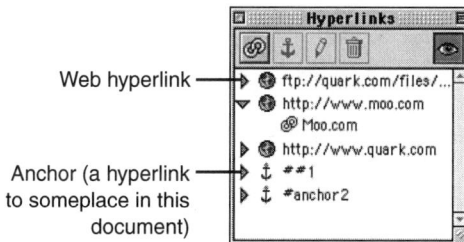

Web hyperlink — ftp://quark.com/files/...
http://www.moo.com
Moo.com
http://www.quark.com
Anchor (a hyperlink ##1
to someplace in this #anchor2
document)

Edit Hyperlink

Mac: Cmd+click on hyperlink

Windows: Ctrl+hyperlink

Mouse: Click the Edit (Pencil) button

Go to URL

Both: Double-click on hyperlink

This feature only works if you have set up a default Web browser in the Preferences dialog box (Edit→Preferences).

Layers Palette

Move Layer Position

Mac: Option+drag layer

Windows: Alt+drag layer

Assign Object to Layer

Both: Drag layer icon to layer

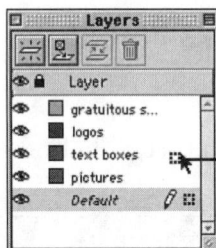

Drag the icon to assign a layer.

Other Palettes

Show/Hide Lists Palette

Menu: View→Show/Hide Lists

Mac: Option+F11

Windows: Ctrl+F11

The Lists palette lets you build a table of contents. You have to make a custom List first (Edit→Lists). If you want a table of contents for all the documents in a book, each document has to have the same List in it. You can use the Book palette's Synchronize button to propagate your List.

Show/Hide Trap Information Palette

Menu: View→Show/Hide Trap Information

Mac: Option+F12

Windows: Ctrl+F12

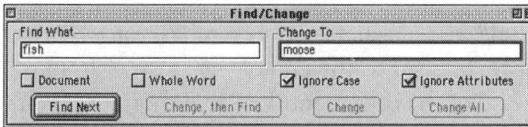

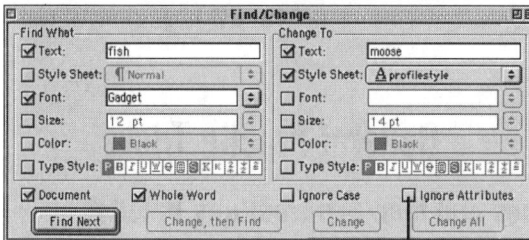

Show Find/Change Palette

Menu: Edit→Find/Change

Mac: Cmd+F

Windows: Ctrl+F

When the Ignore Attributes
check box is turned off, you can
make many more changes to
text. Finding and changing text
color is new in XPress 5.

When the Ignore Attributes check box is turned off, you can make many more changes to text. Finding and changing text color is new in XPress 5.

Palettes

Hide Find/Change Palette

Mac: Cmd+Option+F

Windows: Ctrl+Alt+F

Although Find/Change is now a palette (it was a dialog box in XPress 3), it still takes screen real estate and so I often want to close it.

Change Find Next to Find First

Mac: Option key

Windows: Alt key

The Find/Change palette only searches from the current position of your text cursor to the end of the story, or from the current page to the end of the document. Use this shortcut if you want XPress to search from the beginning of the story. If the Document check-box is on, XPress searches from the beginning of the document.

General Palette Tricks

Apply Changes and then Exit from Any Palette

Mac: Enter or Return

Windows: Enter

Mouse: Click anywhere outside palette

Undo All Changes in a Palette (But Leave Field Active)

Mac: Cmd+Z

Windows: Ctrl+Z

This is the one to remember when you type something totally wrong, like **qwp** instead of **12p**. Also, I find this useful when I type a number into the rotate field of the Modify dialog box or Measurements palette, and XPress tells me that this number would position the item off the pasteboard.

Undo All Changes in a Palette (and Exit the Palette)

Mac: Cmd+period or Esc

Windows: Esc

Jump to Next Field in Palette

Both: Tab

If you use the Columns field in the Measurements palette a lot, you can get really fast at typing Cmd+Option+M (Mac) or Ctrl+Alt+M (Windows) and then five tabs in a row. It's not quite as good as jumping right to the field, but it's much faster than using the mouse to select it.

Jump to Previous Field in Palette

Both: Shift+Tab

Math in the Palettes

Both: Type +, -, *, or / in an equation in any field of any palette.

Using math in the palettes is one of the most powerful features in XPress for precision work. If you want a box to be half as wide, type **/2** after the value in the width field in the Measurements palette. If you want it to be 40-percent taller, type ***1.4** after the value in the Height field. If you want to turn a vignette around to blend in the opposite direction, type **+180** after the value in the degree field of the Colors palette.

You can also mix and match measurements systems. So, for instance, you could set the X field of the Measurements palette to **4p+3cm-2"*6**. Note that QuarkXPress always performs multiplication and division first in these sorts of equations.

Interface

The XPress Environment

Help

Mac:	Help or Cmd+?
Windows:	F1

Environment Dialog Box

Mac:	Option+Help or Cmd+Option+Ctrl+E
Windows:	Ctrl+About QuarkXPress

The Environment dialog box displays information about your copy of XPress as well as the environment in which you're using it. For example, if you need to find your serial number or what printer driver version you're using, check out this dialog box.

If you click the Use Reg. Info button in the Environment dialog box, the program builds a new document, and fills a text box with the same information that was sent to Quark when you registered your copy of XPress.

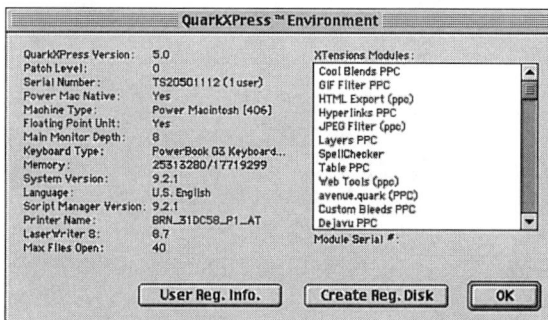

Open Document with New Text Flow

> **Mac:** Option+click Open
>
> **Windows:** Alt+click Open

Each version of QuarkXPress has slightly different methods of flowing text (Quark claims each new version is slightly better, of course). If you hold down the Option/Alt key when clicking the Open button in the Open dialog box, you force the program to reflow the text according to the current version's rules. It's rare that you'll see much, if any, difference. I've found, however, that this sometimes clears up the occasional unexplainable text reflow weirdness. Some people make it a habit to always open old legacy documents with this shortcut, but be aware that your text might reflow if you do.

Open XTensions Manager

> **Both:** Spacebar at launch

Remember that XPress lets you turn XTensions on or off only when you launch the program. Because I have a number of XTensions, I may use this shortcut several times a day, quitting and relaunching with the spacebar held down each time I want to use a different set of XTensions. (Maybe it's just superstitious, but I get nervous when I have too many XTensions loaded at the same time.) By the way, you often have to wait at least half a second or so after you launch the program before you hold down the spacebar; then keep it held down until you see the XTensions Manager dialog box.

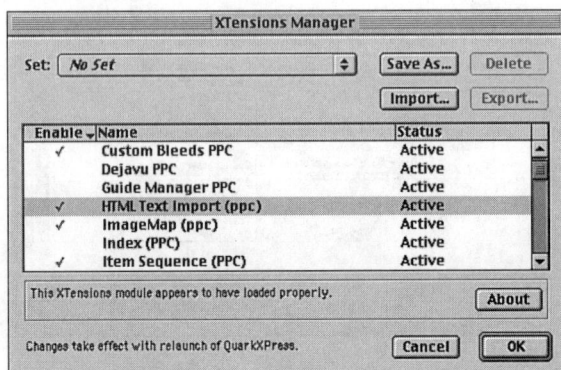

XTensions Manager		
Set: *No Set* ⬦	Save As...	Delete
	Import...	Export...

Enable ▾	Name	Status	
✓	Custom Bleeds PPC	Active	▲
	Dejavu PPC	Active	
	Guide Manager PPC	Active	
✓	HTML Text Import (ppc)	Active	
✓	ImageMap (ppc)	Active	
	Index (PPC)	Active	
✓	Item Sequence (PPC)	Active	▼

This XTensions module appears to have loaded properly. [About]

Changes take effect with relaunch of QuarkXPress. [Cancel] [OK]

Interface

Change Document Window

Mac: Shift+click on title bar

Windows users don't need this feature because QuarkXPress for
Windows has a menu called Windows, which offers the same func-
tionality. You can Shift+click anywhere on the title bar to get this.

Note that the Window menu also offers Tile Documents and
Stack Documents. When you hold down Option/Alt and then
select either of these, XPress automatically changes all the documents to Thumbnails view at the same time. This saves time
when you have two documents open and you want to drag pages
from one into the other.

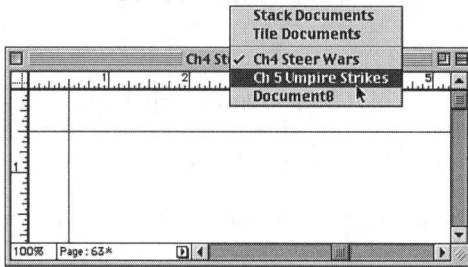

Interrupt Screen Redraw

Mac: Cmd+click (period)

Windows: Esc

This only works when you have turned off the Off-Screen draw
feature in the Application Preferences dialog box. When that feature is turned on, you can't see individual objects drawing on the
screen.

Note that QuarkXPress only interrupts the screen redraw when the
current object, such as whatever object is drawing when you press
this shortcut, is finished displaying onscreen.

Force Screen Redraw

Mac: Cmd+Option+. (period)

Windows: Shift+Esc

QuarkXPress has some funky screen redraw problems, and every now and again you'll see something onscreen that you know isn't really there—such as boxes that you deleted, or lines that you've moved elsewhere. These problems almost always go away as soon as you force QuarkXPress to redraw the page.

Selecting Items

Select Through Objects

Mac: Cmd+Shift+Option+click

Windows: Ctrl+Shift+Alt+click

If there are more than two objects stacked, this will successively select deeper and deeper. If you want to drag an object to move it after selecting it, don't let go of the mouse button.

Select or Deselect Multiple Objects or Points on a Path

Both: Shift+click

Sometimes the best way to select a group of objects is to press Cmd+A (Mac) or Ctrl+A (Windows) to select everything on a page when the Item tool is selected; then Shift+click to deselect the objects you *don't* want.

Deselect All Objects

Both: Tab

This always works when you have the Item tool selected. If you have the Content tool selected, it only works when more than one object is selected.

Dialog Boxes

OK Button

Mac:	Return or Enter
Windows:	Enter

Cancel Button

Mac:	Cmd+Period or Esc
Windows:	Esc

Apply Button

Mac:	Cmd+A
Windows:	Alt+A

Apply is great if you want to preview the changes that you've made to a dialog box before clicking OK. If you don't like the changes, you can change the values and select Apply again, or just click Cancel to revert back to the original state.

Continuous Apply

Mac:	Cmd+Option+A or Option+Click-Apply
Windows:	Alt+Click-Apply

If you find yourself using the Apply button frequently or pressing Cmd/Ctrl+A a lot, consider turning on Continuous Apply. When it's on, everything you do in a dialog box gets applied immediately. Of course, you can still click Cancel if you don't like the changes. This shortcut turns Continuous Apply both on and off. Unfortunately, Continuous Apply only works in the features found under the Style menu (like Paragraph Formats). It doesn't work in features found in other menus, such as the Modify dialog box.

By the way, when Continuous Apply is on when you make a change to a field, such as a measurement in the Modify dialog box, you have to select a different field by clicking or by pressing Tab before XPress recognizes that you're ready to have the change applied.

Interface

Yes Button

Mac: Cmd+Y

Windows: Y

No Button

Mac: Cmd+N

Windows: N

I use this all the time when I close a document without wanting to save my changes.

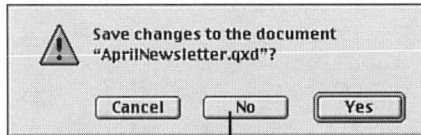

Alternately, press N (Windows) or Cmd + N (Mac)

Jump to Next Field in Dialog Box

Both: Tab

Jump to Previous Field in Dialog Box

Both: Shift+Tab

Interface

Switch to Next Tab in a Tabbed Dialog Box

Mac: Cmd+Tab

Windows: Ctrl+Tab

Type Cmd + Tab (Mac) or Ctrl + Tab (Windows) to switch
to the next tab in these kinds of dialog boxes.

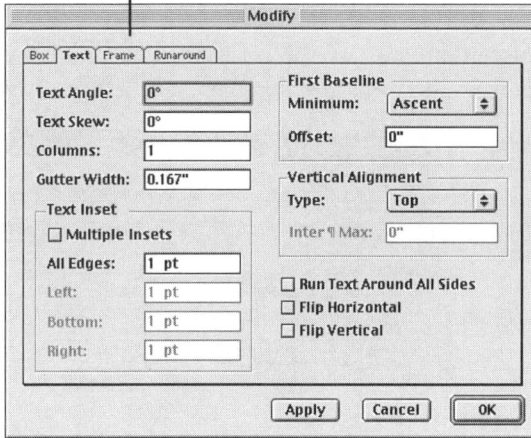

```
┌──────────────────────── Modify ────────────────────────┐
│                                                          │
│ ┌Box │ Text │ Frame │ Runaround ┐                        │
│                                                          │
│  Text Angle:   [0°        ]    ┌First Baseline────────┐  │
│                                │ Minimum:  [Ascent ▲▼]│  │
│  Text Skew:    [0°        ]    │                      │  │
│  Columns:      [1         ]    │ Offset:   [0"        ]│  │
│  Gutter Width: [0.167"    ]    └──────────────────────┘  │
│ ┌Text Inset───────────────┐   ┌Vertical Alignment────┐  │
│ │ ☐ Multiple Insets       │   │ Type:     [Top    ▲▼]│  │
│ │ All Edges:    [1 pt     ]│   │ Inter ¶ Max: [0"     ]│  │
│ │ Left:         [1 pt     ]│   └──────────────────────┘  │
│ │ Bottom:       [1 pt     ]│   ☐ Run Text Around All Sides│
│ │ Right:        [1 pt     ]│   ☐ Flip Horizontal         │
│ └─────────────────────────┘   ☐ Flip Vertical            │
│                                                          │
│               [ Apply ] [ Cancel ] [  OK  ]              │
└──────────────────────────────────────────────────────────┘
```

Switch to Previous Tab in a Tabbed Dialog Box

Mac: Cmd+Shift+Tab

Windows: Ctrl+Shift+Tab

Undo Changes in a Dialog Box

Mac: Cmd+Z or F1

Windows: Ctrl+Shift+Z

This resets all the changes you've made in a dialog box back to the
original state of the dialog box when you opened it.

Undo Current Change in Dialog Box

Windows: Ctrl+Shift+Z

This resets the change you have made to the current field in the
dialog box. There is currently no Macintosh equivalent.

Interface

Tabs and Rulers

Open Tabs Dialog Box

Menu: Style→Tabs

Mac: Cmd+Shift+T

Windows: Ctrl+Shift+T

Note that you can also get to this dialog box by opening the Paragraph Formats dialog box and then choosing the Tabs tab.

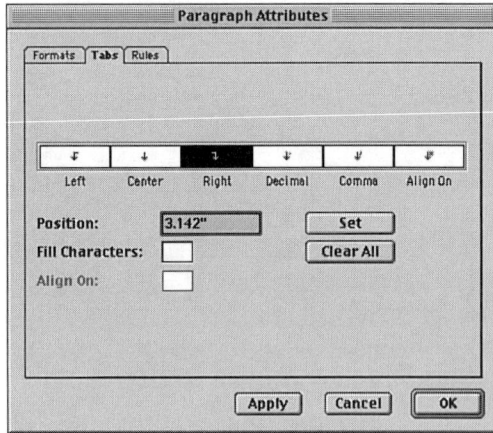

This ruler appears when the Tabs dialog box is open.

Delete All Tab Stops

Mac: Option+click in Tab ruler

Windows: Alt+click in Tab ruler

Mouse: Click Clear All button

The Tab ruler is only visible when the Paragraph Formats dialog box is open.

Set Tab Stop in Dialog Box

Mac: Cmd+S

Windows: Alt+S

Cmd+S on the Macintosh is ordinarily the same as selecting File→Save, of course. However, when the Tabs dialog box is open, it means *set* a tab stop at whatever measurement you type in the Position field.

Note that selecting Apply—or better yet, pressing Cmd+A (Mac) or Ctrl+A (Windows)—will both set the tab stop *and* apply it to the currently selected paragraphs.

Show/Hide Guides

Menu: View→Show/Hide Guides

Both: F7

I am asked about a shortcut for hiding guides in my workshops all the time. The answer is embarrassingly simple: The F7 key.

Delete All Guides

Mac: Option+click in ruler

Windows: Alt+click in ruler

Option+clicking when the pasteboard is touching the ruler deletes pasteboard guides. With the page touching, it deletes page guides.

Interface

Menus

File Menu

The File menu enables you to control anything related to saving or opening files to disk, such as creating new documents, opening documents from disk, importing text or pictures from disk, and so on.

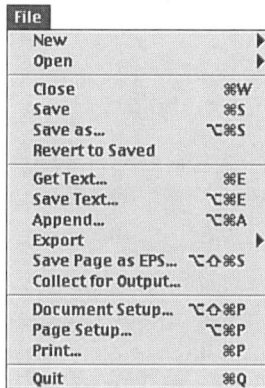

File	
New	▶
Open	▶
Close	⌘W
Save	⌘S
Save as...	⌥⌘S
Revert to Saved	
Get Text...	⌘E
Save Text...	⌥⌘E
Append...	⌥⌘A
Export	▶
Save Page as EPS...	⌥⇧⌘S
Collect for Output...	
Document Setup...	⌥⇧⌘P
Page Setup...	⌥⌘P
Print...	⌘P
Quit	⌘Q

New Document

Menu: File→New→Document

Mac: Cmd+N

Windows: Ctrl+N

QuarkXPress remembers the settings in the New Document dialog box and uses them the next time you create a document.

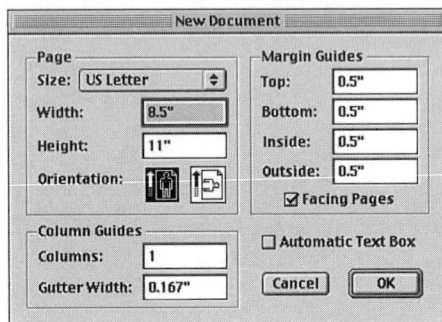

New Library

Menu: File→New→Library

Mac: Cmd+Option+N

Windows: Ctrl+Alt+N

Libraries are a great way to keep track of page items that you'll use more than once. One of my favorite tricks is to apply special colors, such as Pantone colors, or colors that a particular client often uses, to objects and then drag those objects into a library. The next time you need those colors, it's faster to pull those items from the library than it is to recreate the colors from scratch. This also works with style sheets, H&J settings, and custom dashes and stripes.

New Web Document

Menu: File→New→Web Document

Mac: Cmd+Option+Shift+N

Windows: Ctrl+Alt+Shift+N

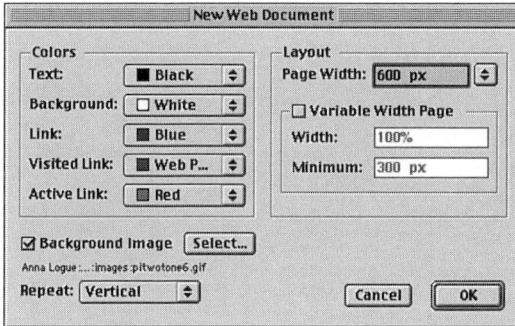

```
┌──────────────────── New Web Document ────────────────────┐
│ ┌─Colors────────────────┐  ┌─Layout──────────────────┐   │
│ │ Text:        ■ Black ⬍│  │ Page Width: 600 px    ⬍ │   │
│ │ Background: □ White  ⬍│  │  ┌─☐ Variable Width Page─┐│   │
│ │ Link:        ■ Blue  ⬍│  │  │ Width:   100%         ││   │
│ │ Visited Link: ■ Web P...⬍│ │ Minimum: 300 px       ││   │
│ │ Active Link:  ■ Red  ⬍│  │  └───────────────────────┘│   │
│ └───────────────────────┘  └─────────────────────────┘   │
│  ☑ Background Image  [ Select... ]                        │
│  Anna Logue:...:images:pitwotone6.gif                     │
│  Repeat: Vertical ⬍              [ Cancel ]  [  OK  ]     │
└──────────────────────────────────────────────────────────┘
```

New XML Document

Menu: File→New→XML Document

Both: Cmd+Shift+X

Windows: Ctrl+Shift+X

You must choose an XMT template and a DTD file to open an XML document. DTD files lay out the structure of an XML file.

Open

Menu: File→Open

Mac: Cmd+O

Windows: Ctrl+O

Menus

Close

Menu:	File→Close
Mac:	Cmd+W
Windows:	Ctrl+F4

If XPress asks you whether you want to save changes, remember that N means **No**, Esc means **Cancel**, and pressing Enter means **OK**.

Close All Documents

Mac:	Cmd+Option+W
Windows:	Alt+W then press A

Save

Menu:	File→Save
Mac:	Cmd+S
Windows:	Ctrl+S

Save As

Menu:	File→Save As
Mac:	Cmd+Option+S
Windows:	Ctrl+Alt+S

Just because XPress lets you save your document in an earlier version doesn't mean you should. You'll lose all the new features! For instance, if you put text on a path, the text gets converted into a regular text box. If you're on a Macintosh, try to remember to add the .qxd file extension to your document names. It's a bi-platform world these days, and you need that extension to be able to use the file in Windows.

QuarkXPress Save As
dialog box for Macintosh

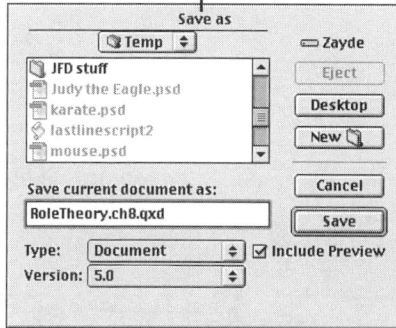

QuarkXPress Save As
dialog box for Windows

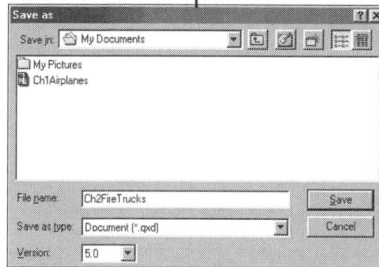

Revert to Last Auto Save

Mac: Option+Revert to Saved

Windows: Alt+Revert to Saved

The Revert to Saved feature always returns your document back to
its state the last time you saved. But if you have Auto Save turned
on in Application Preferences (Edit→Preferences), this shortcut
returns you to the last time XPress performed an Auto Save. If you
saved 20 minutes ago and Auto Save happened four minutes ago,
this might be very useful.

Menus

Get Text/Picture

Menu: File→Get Text or File→Get Picture

Mac: Cmd+E

Windows: Ctrl+E

QuarkXPress lets you import a picture into a picture box with either the Item or the Content tools, but you must use the Content tool to import text into a text box.

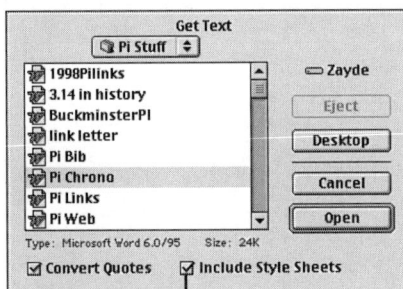

Always turn the Import Styles check box on when you import MS Word documents.

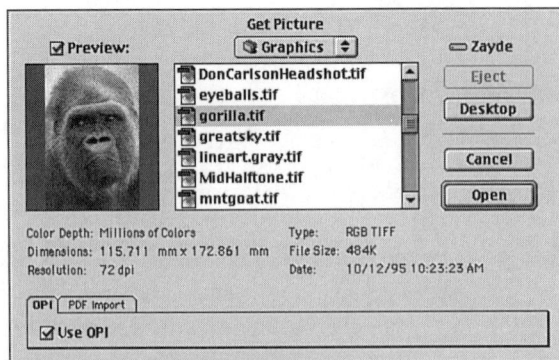

Save Text

Menu: File→Save Text

Mac: Cmd+Option+E

Windows: Ctrl+Alt+E

You must have a text box selected with the Content tool.

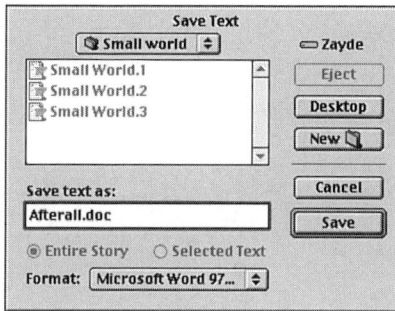

Document Setup

Menu: File→Document Setup

Mac: Cmd+Option+Shift+P

Windows: Ctrl+Alt+Shift+P

People are often disappointed when they look here to change their margins. No can do! To change your page margins, go to the master page and then select Page→Margins.

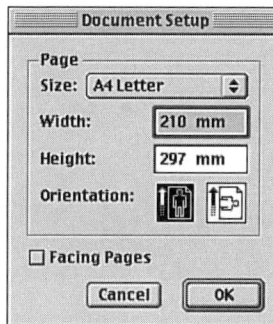

Menus

Append

Menu: File→Append

Mac: Cmd+Option+A

Windows: Ctrl+Alt+A

Have you created a style sheet, color, or other setting in a document that you want to copy into another document? You can use the Append feature to pull it over. Bonus tip: If you use Append when no documents are open, you can add a style sheet, color, custom dash or stripe, or H&J setting to every new document you create from then on.

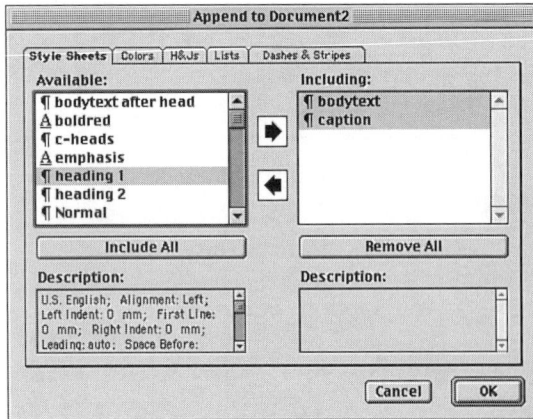

Save Page As EPS

Menu: File→Save Page As EPS

Mac: Cmd+Option+Shift+S

Windows: Ctrl+Alt+Shift+S

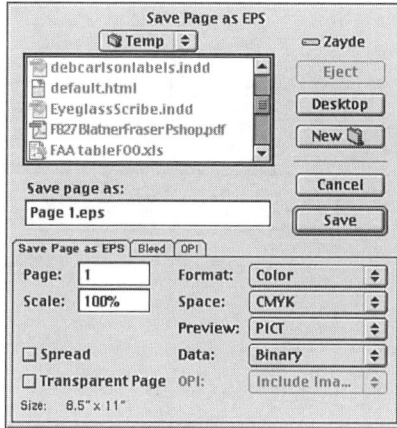

Page Setup

Menu: File→Page Setup

Mac: Cmd+Option+P

Windows: Ctrl+Alt+P

This does the same thing as selecting Print and then skipping to the Setup tab in the dialog box.

Print

Menu: File→Print

Mac: Cmd+P

Windows: Ctrl+P

Don't forget you can use Cmd+Tab (Mac) or Ctrl+Tab (Windows) to move through the various tabs in this dialog box.

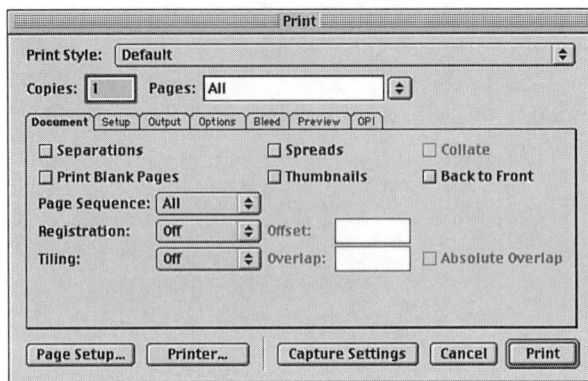

Quit

Menu:	File→Quit
Mac:	Cmd+Q
Windows:	Ctrl+Q or Alt+Shift+F4

I often have to use software before it gets released to the public, called beta software. Once upon a time, I was using a beta version of XPress and I noticed something weird. The Quit feature was missing from the File menu! My officemate and I looked at each other, laughed, and said "Why would anyone want to Quit from XPress?" Fortunately, Quark fixed that bug quickly.

Edit Menu

The Edit menu enables you to change preferences, style sheet definitions, colors, and other document variables.

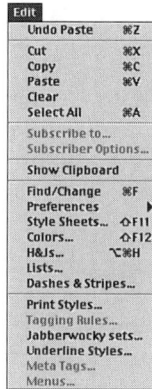

Edit	
Undo Paste	⌘Z
Cut	⌘X
Copy	⌘C
Paste	⌘V
Clear	
Select All	⌘A
Subscribe to...	
Subscriber Options...	
Show Clipboard	
Find/Change	⌘F
Preferences	▶
Style Sheets...	⇧F11
Colors...	⇧F12
H&Js...	⌥⌘H
Lists...	
Dashes & Stripes...	
Print Styles...	
Tagging Rules...	
Jabberwocky sets...	
Underline Styles...	
Meta Tags...	
Menus...	

Undo

Menu: Edit→Undo

Mac: Cmd+Z or F1

Windows: Ctrl+Z

Cut

Menu: Edit→Cut

Mac: Cmd+X or F2

Windows: Ctrl+X

Copy

Menu: Edit→Copy

Mac: Cmd+C or F3

Windows: Ctrl+C

Cut Item with the Content Tool

Mac: Cmd+Option+X

Windows: Ctrl+Alt+X

This is identical to switching to the Item tool, cutting the item to the clipboard, and switching back to the Content tool or whatever other tool you had selected. It's most handy when you're copying or cutting a box or line that you intend to paste into a text box as an anchored object.

Copy Item with the Content Tool

Mac: Cmd+Option+C

Windows: Ctrl+Alt+C

This is identical to switching to the Item tool, copying the item, and switching back to the Content tool or whatever other tool you had selected.

Paste

Menu: Edit→Paste

Mac: Cmd+V or F4

Windows: Ctrl+V

I wish there were a feature called "Paste in the same place on the page that it was when I cut it," but there isn't. Oh well.

Select All

Menu: Edit→Select All

Mac: Cmd+A

Windows: Ctrl+A

When a text box is selected with the Content tool, this shortcut selects all the text in the box. When the Item tool is selected, it selects all the items on a page spread, or a single page, in the case of a single-sided document.

Find/Change

Menu: Edit→Find/Change

Mac: Cmd+F

Windows: Ctrl+F

Close Find/Change Palette

Mac: Cmd+Option+F

Windows: Ctrl+Alt+F

Find Next

Both: Return (Enter)

Of course, pressing Return (Mac) or Enter (both) ordinarily types a character wherever your cursor is. However, when the focus is on the Find/Change palette, this keystroke engages the Find Next button. How do you know if the focus is on the palette? In XPress 4, the focus is on the palette when the Find Next button is high-lighted. In XPress 5, the Find or the Change fields are highlighted. It's a subtle difference, but you'll see it quickly once you've tried it once or twice. You can always re-highlight the button by pressing Cmd+F (Mac) or Ctrl+F (Windows).

Find First

Mac: Option+Return or Option+Enter

Windows: Alt+Enter

The Option/Alt key always changes the Find Next button in the Find/Change palette to a Find First button.

Menus

Document Preferences

Menu: Edit→Preferences→Preferences

Mac: Cmd+Y

Windows: Ctrl+Y

Document Preferences in XPress 4

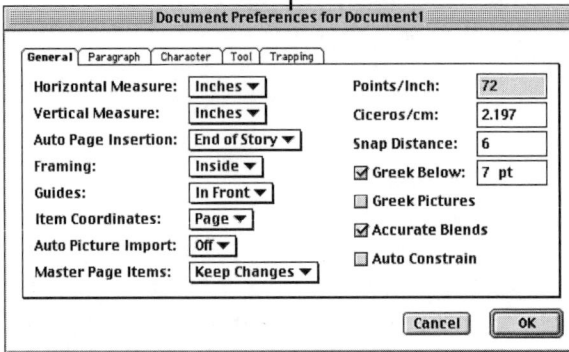

Document Preferences in XPress 5

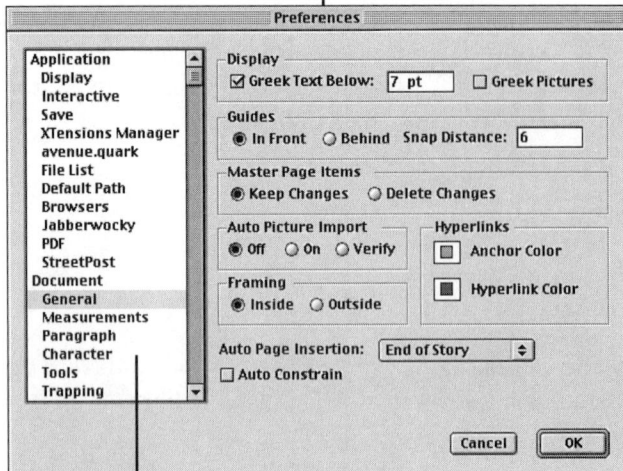

You can switch to the other tabs by pressing
the Up Arrow and Down Arrow keys.

Paragraph Preferences

Mac: Cmd+Option+Y

Windows: Ctrl+Alt+Y

This is the same as opening the Document Preferences dialog box, and switching to the Paragraph tab.

Application Preferences

Menu: Edit→Preferences→Application (in version 4)

Mac: Cmd+Option+Shift+Y

Windows: Ctrl+Alt+Shift+Y

In XPress 5, this is the same as opening the Preferences dialog box, and switching to the Display tab.

Trapping Preferences

Mac: Option+Shift+F12

Windows: Ctrl+Shift+F12

In XPress 5, this is the same as opening the Preferences dialog box, and switching to the Trapping tab.

Style Sheets Dialog Box

Menu: Edit→Style Sheets

Mac: Shift+F11

Windows: Shift+F11

Colors Dialog Box

Menu: Edit→Colors

Mac: Shift+F12

Windows: Shift+F12

H&Js Settings Dialog Box

Menu: Edit→H&Js

Mac: Cmd+Option+H or Option+Shift+F11

Windows: Ctrl+Shift+F11

H&Js stands for hyphenation and justification settings. This is where you can turn hyphenation on and off, or change the way the XPress adds letter and word spacing to justify paragraphs.

Subscriber Options

Menu: Edit→Subscriber Options

Mac: Double-click with Content tool

Subscriber Options is a feature of the Macintosh operating system, so it's not available in Windows. You can use Subscriber Options even with TIFF and EPS files. I use this frequently after editing a picture. For example, say you edit a photo in Photoshop or Illustrator. Instead of re-importing it into XPress or using the Usage dialog box to update the version in your document, you can double-click on the image with the Content tool and then click the Get Edition Now button.

When you click Open Publisher, the original program (Photoshop, or Illustrator, or whatever) should launch and then open that image. However, this sometimes stops working. It's an operating system glitch, not an XPress bug.

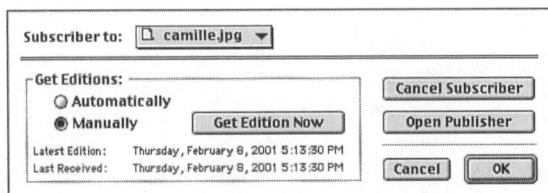

Menus

Style Menu

The Style menu changes depending on what you have selected:
a text box, a picture box, or a line.

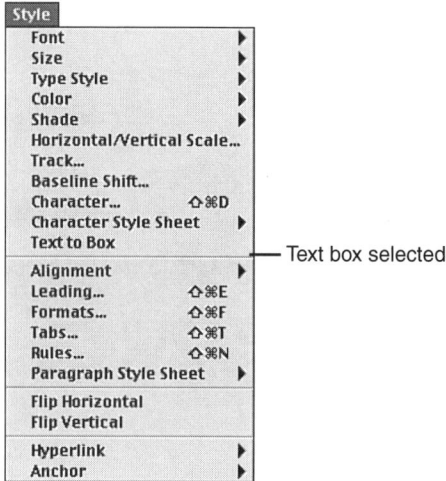

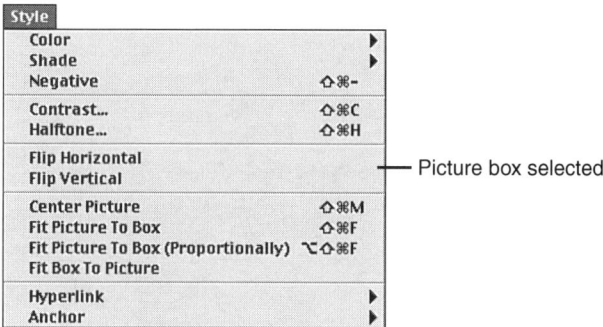

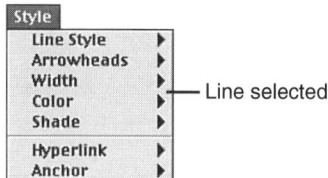

Style	
Font	▶
Size	▶
Type Style	▶
Color	▶
Shade	▶
Horizontal/Vertical Scale...	
Track...	
Baseline Shift...	
Character...	⇧⌘D
Character Style Sheet	▶
Text to Box	
Alignment	▶
Leading...	⇧⌘E
Formats...	⇧⌘F
Tabs...	⇧⌘T
Rules...	⇧⌘N
Paragraph Style Sheet	▶
Flip Horizontal	
Flip Vertical	
Hyperlink	▶
Anchor	▶

—— Text box selected

Style	
Color	▶
Shade	▶
Negative	⇧⌘-
Contrast...	⇧⌘C
Halftone...	⇧⌘H
Flip Horizontal	
Flip Vertical	
Center Picture	⇧⌘M
Fit Picture To Box	⇧⌘F
Fit Picture To Box (Proportionally)	⌥⇧⌘F
Fit Box To Picture	
Hyperlink	▶
Anchor	▶

—— Picture box selected

Style	
Line Style	▶
Arrowheads	▶
Width	▶
Color	▶
Shade	▶
Hyperlink	▶
Anchor	▶

—— Line selected

Menus

Character Attributes

Menu:	Style→Character
Mac:	Cmd+Shift+D
Windows:	Ctrl+Shift+D

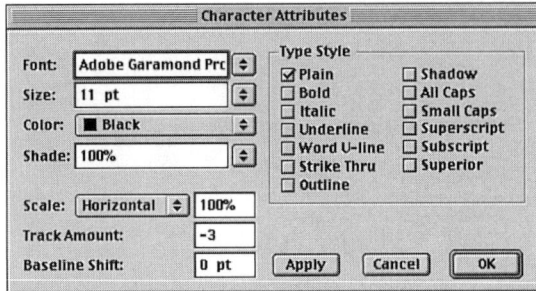

Other Size

Menu:	Style→Size→Other
Mac:	Cmd+Shift+ \
Windows:	Ctrl+Shift+ \

This is the same as opening the Character Attributes dialog box, and pressing Tab to jump to the Size field.

Paragraph Formats

Menu:	Style→Size→Formats
Mac:	Cmd+Shift+F
Windows:	Ctrl+Shift+F

Menus

For some reason, Quark assumes that you'll know that Formats means **Paragraph Formats**. Only beginners select the whole paragraph before applying paragraph formatting—power users just place the cursor anywhere in the paragraph. XPress is smart enough to apply the formatting to the whole paragraph even if only a portion of the paragraph is selected.

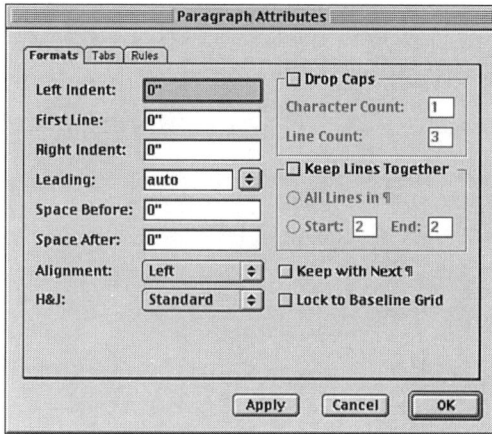

Leading

Menu:	Style→Leading
Mac:	Cmd+Shift+E
Windows:	Ctrl+Shift+E

This is the same as opening the Paragraph Formats dialog box and pressing Tab three times to jump to the Leading field.

Tabs

Menu:	Style→Tabs
Mac:	Cmd+Shift+T
Windows:	Ctrl+Shift+T

This is the same as opening the Paragraph Formats dialog box and switching to the Tabs tab.

Paragraph Rules

Menu: Style→Rules

Mac: Cmd+Shift+N

Windows: Ctrl+Shift+N

This is the same as opening the Paragraph Formats dialog box and switching to the Rules tab.

Negative

Menu: Style→Negative

Mac: Cmd+Shift+hyphen

Windows: Ctrl+Shift+hyphen

Negative works only when you have a grayscale or black-and-white TIFF selected in a picture box. It literally turns white into black and black into white.

Contrast

Menu: Style→Contrast

Mac: Cmd+Shift+C

Windows: Ctrl+Shift+C

The Other Contrast dialog box lets you apply Photoshop-like contrast curves to your TIFF images. However, it's a *very* blunt instrument, and I can't recommend you use it except for perhaps rough drafts for a client.

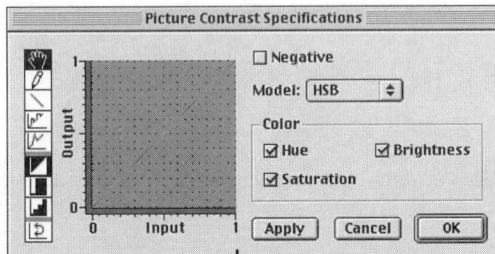

This looks more useful than it really is.

Halftone

Menu:	Style→Halftone
Mac:	Cmd+Shift+H
Windows:	Ctrl+Shift+H

QuarkXPress lets you apply a custom halftone screen to a grayscale TIFF image, which is occasionally useful when creating special effects. In XPress 5, however, you can no longer see what the halftone will look like, which makes this feature especially problematic. I'd just do custom halftones in Photoshop if I were you.

Center Picture

Menu:	Style→Center Picture (XPress 5 only)
Mac:	Cmd+Shift+M
Windows:	Ctrl+Shift+M

This keyboard shortcut has been in XPress for years, but now it's listed in the Style menu, too.

Fit Picture to Box

Menu:	Style→Fit Picture to Box (XPress 5 only)
Mac:	Cmd+Shift+F
Windows:	Ctrl+Shift+F

This keyboard shortcut has been in XPress for years, but now it's listed in the Style menu, too. Note that this usually stretches your picture disproportionately, so I rarely use it.

Fit Picture to Box (Proportionally)

Menu:	Style→Fit Picture to Box Proportionally (XPress 5 only)
Mac:	Cmd+Option+Shift+F
Windows:	Ctrl+Alt+Shift+F

Menus

This keyboard shortcut has been in XPress for years, but now it's also listed in the Style menu. Remember that when you make a bitmapped graphic larger in Xpress, the image resolution goes down!

Item Menu

There are four kinds of items in QuarkXPress: picture boxes, text boxes, tables, and lines. Any time you need to manipulate an item on your page, the Item menu is a pretty good place to start.

```
Item
Modify...              ⌘M
Frame...               ⌘B
Runaround...           ⌘T
Clipping...           ⌥⌘T
Duplicate              ⌘D
Step and Repeat...    ⌥⌘D
Delete                 ⌘K
Group                  ⌘G
Ungroup                ⌘U
Constrain
Lock                   F6
Merge                   ▶
Split                   ▶
Send to Back          ⇧F5
Bring to Front         F5
Space/Align...         ⌘,
Shape                   ▶
Content                 ▶
Edit                    ▶
Point/Segment Type      ▶
Delete All Hot Areas
Convert Text to Table...
Table                   ▶
Gridlines               ▶
Rollover                ▶
```

Modify (Item Specifications)

Menu:	Item→Modify
Mac:	Cmd+M or Cmd+double-click
Windows:	Ctrl+M or Ctrl+double-click

You can double-click on the object without the Cmd (Mac) or Ctrl (Windows) key if you already have the Item tool selected.

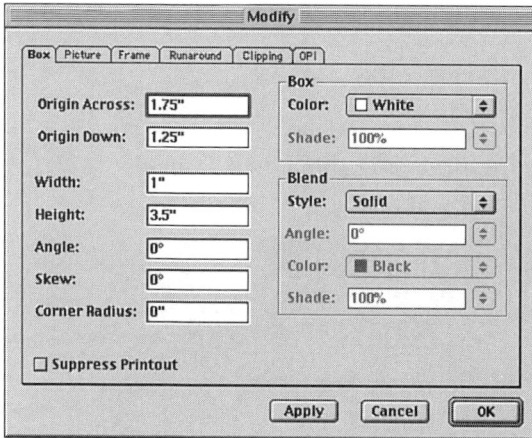

Frame

Menu: Item→Frame

Mac: Cmd+B

Windows: Ctrl+B

This is the same as opening the Modify dialog box and switching to the Frame tab.

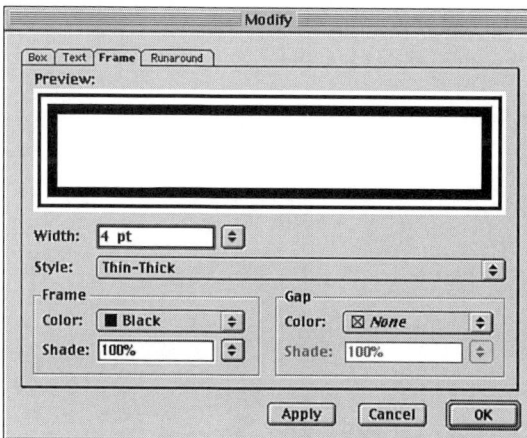

Runaround

Menu: Item→Runaround

Mac: Cmd+T

Windows: Ctrl+T

This is the same as opening the Modify dialog box and switching to the Runaround tab.

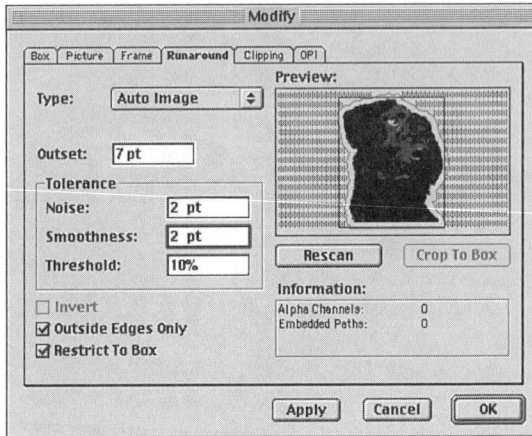

Clipping

Menu: Item→Clipping

Mac: Cmd+Option+T

Windows: Ctrl+Alt+T

This is the same as opening the Modify dialog box, and switching to the Clipping tab.

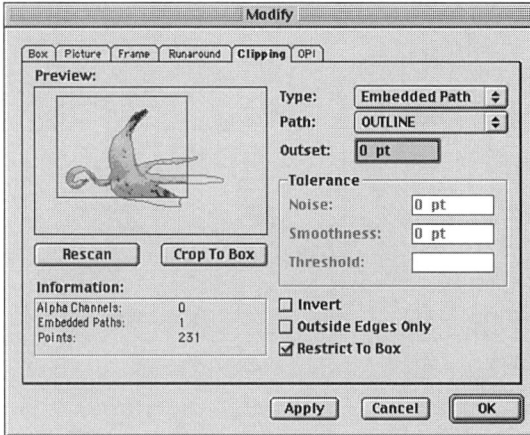

Duplicate

Menu: Item→Duplicate

Mac: Cmd+D

Windows: Ctrl+D

Remember that Duplicate always uses the same offset values as you last specified in the Step and Repeat dialog box, or .25 inches or 2p6 if you haven't used Step and Repeat yet.

Step and Repeat

Menu: Item→Step and Repeat

Mac: Cmd+Option+D

Windows: Ctrl+Alt+D

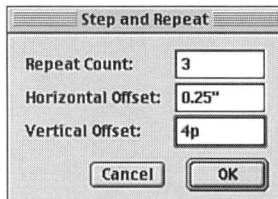

Menus

Delete

Menu:	Item→Delete
Mac:	Cmd+K
Windows:	Ctrl+K

Group

Menu:	Item→Group
Mac:	Cmd+G
Windows:	Ctrl+G

Ungroup

Menu:	Item→Ungroup
Mac:	Cmd+U
Windows:	Ctrl+U

Lock/Unlock

Menu:	Item→Lock/Unlock
Both:	F6

When you lock an object, it's not as locked as you think it is. The only thing Lock does is stop you from dragging the object around accidentally. You can still move it with the Arrow keys with the Item tool selected, or in the Measurements palette or in several other ways.

Space/Align

    Menu: Item→Space/Align

    Mac: Cmd+, (comma)

    Windows: Ctrl+, (comma)

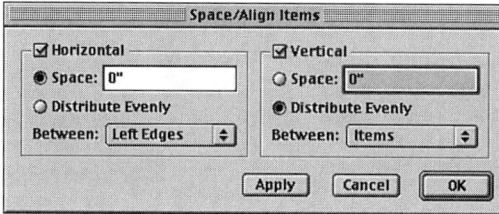

Space/Align Items	
☑ Horizontal	**☑ Vertical**
● Space: [0"]	○ Space: [0"]
○ Distribute Evenly	● Distribute Evenly
Between: [Left Edges ⬍]	Between: [Items ⬍]

                                     [Apply] [Cancel] [OK]

Bring to Front

    Menu: Item→Bring to Front

    Both: F5

Move Forward

    Menu: Item→Bring Forward

    Mac: Option+F5

    Windows: Ctrl+F5

For some obscure reason, on the Macintosh you have to hold down the Option key in order to see the Move Forward feature in the Item menu.

Send to Back

    Menu: Item→Send to Back

    Both: Shift+F5

Move Backward

Menu: Item→Send Backward

Mac: Option+Shift+F5

Windows: Ctrl+Shift+F5

I don't know why, but on the Mac you have to hold down the Option key to be able to see the Move Backward feature in the Item menu.

Edit Shape

Menu: Item→Edit→Shape

Mac: Shift+F4

Windows: F10

When you first build a bézier shape or convert text to paths, XPress shows you all the points along the path. If you want the bounding box instead (the regular corner and side handles), turn off Edit Shape. When you want the points again, select this again.

Edit Runaround

Menu: Item→Edit→Runaround

Mac: Option+F4

Windows: Ctrl+F10

Edit Runaround is a toggle. When you press this keystroke, you either turn the feature on or off. Edit Runaround lets you edit the runaround path for a selected graphic, but only when you have turned text wrap on in the Runaround dialog box.

Edit Clipping Path

Menu: Item→Edit→Clipping Path

Mac: Option+Shift+F4

Windows: Ctrl+Shift+F10

Menus

Don't like the clipping path around your TIFF image? You can edit it after pressing this keystroke. QuarkXPress lets you do this with EPS images, too, but the results aren't always what you expect. I suggest you stick to TIFF images here.

Change to Corner Point

Menu:	Item→Point/Segment Type→Corner Point
Mac:	Option+F1
Windows:	Ctrl+F1

I almost never use this item (or the next four) because it's usually just easier to adjust points and segments using the Measurements palette. Nevertheless, it's nice to know they're here.

Change to Smooth Point

Menu:	Item→Point/Segment Type→Smooth Point
Mac:	Option+F2
Windows:	Ctrl+F2

Change to Symmetrical Point

Menu:	Item→Point/Segment Type→Symmetrical Point
Mac:	Option+F3
Windows:	Ctrl+F3

Change to Straight Segment

Menu:	Item→Point/Segment Type→Straight Segment
Mac:	Option+Shift+F1
Windows:	Ctrl+Shift+F1

Menus

Change to Curved Segment

Menu: Item→Point/Segment Type→Curved Segment

Mac: Option+Shift+F2

Windows: Ctrl+Shift+F2

Page Menu

The Page menu enables you to control whole pages, such as navigating to a specific page, adding or removing pages, and so on.

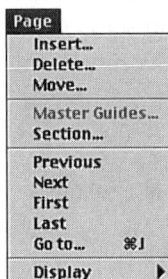

```
Page
  Insert...
  Delete...
  Move...
  Master Guides...
  Section...
  Previous
  Next
  First
  Last
  Go to...      ⌘J
  Display          ▶
```

Go To Page

Menu: Page→Go To

Mac: Cmd+J

Windows: Ctrl+J

If you have used the Section feature to begin your document on a specific page number, you can type **the fifth page** into the Go To dialog box by typing **+5**. The Plus sign makes it an absolute number. Cool, huh?

Toggle Displaying Master Pages

Mac: Shift+F10

Windows: Shift+F4

I wish the Go To dialog box would let you jump to a master page, but it won't. However, this keystroke jumps right to the first master page; then you can use the next two keystrokes to navigate through other master pages, if you have more than one. This is the same thing as double-clicking on the first master page in the Document Layout palette.

Display Next Master Page

Mac:	Option+F10
Windows:	Ctrl+Shift+F4

Display Previous Master Page

Mac:	Option+Shift+F10
Windows:	Ctrl+Shift+F3

Go To First Page

Menu:	Page→First
Mac:	Cmd+Home or Ctrl+Shift+A
Windows:	Ctrl+Page Up

Go To Last Page

Menu:	Page→Last
Mac:	Cmd+End or Ctrl+Shift+D
Windows:	Ctrl+Page Down

Go To Previous Page

Menu:	Page→Previous
Mac:	Shift+Page Up or Ctrl+Shift+K
Windows:	Shift+Page Up

Go To Next Page

Menu: Page→Next

Mac: Shift+Page Down or Ctrl+Shift+L

Windows: Shift+Page Down

Page Properties

Menu: Page→Page Properties

Mac: Cmd+Option+Shift-A

Windows: Ctrl+Alt+Shift-A

You'll only see this item when you have a Web document open.

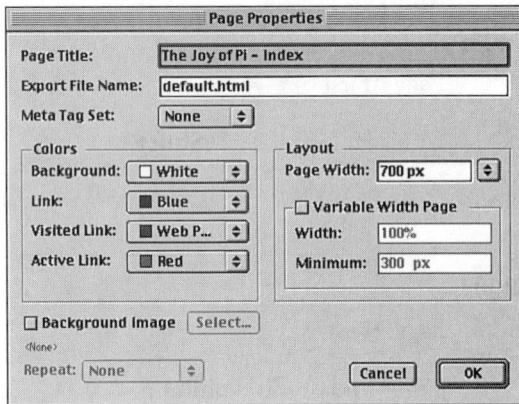

View Menu

Need to open a palette? All the palettes are listed in the View menu, along with controls for how to display your document.

```
View
  Fit in Window          ⌘0
  50%
  75%
✓ Actual Size            ⌘1
  200%
  Thumbnails             ⇧F6
  Windows                ▶
  Hide Guides            F7
  Show Baseline Grid     ⌥F7
✓ Snap to Guides         ⇧F7
  Hide Rulers            ⌘R
  Show Invisibles        ⌘I
  Hide Visual Indicators
  Hide Tools             F8
  Show Measurements      F9
  Show Document Layout   F10
  Show Style Sheets      F11
  Show Colors            F12
  Show Trap Information   ⌥F12
  Show Lists             ⌥F11
  Show Layers
  Show Profile Information
  Show Hyperlinks
  Show Index
  Show Sequences
  Show Placeholders
```

Fit in Window

Menu: View→Fit in Window

Mac: Cmd+Zero

Windows: Ctrl+Zero

QuarkXPress always figures out the proper view percentage to fit the current page in the window.

Fit Pasteboard in Window

Mac: Cmd+Option+Zero

Windows: Ctrl+Alt+Zero

Note that there's no command to fit a page spread in the document window, such as a left- and right-hand page together, so this is as close as it gets.

Menus

Actual Size

Menu: View→Actual Size

Mac: Cmd+1

Windows: Ctrl+1

While QuarkXPress for Windows lets you specify what your screen resolution is, there is unfortunately no way to do this on the Macintosh. That means that Actual Size rarely actually gives you actual, real life size where one inch on screen equals one inch in your final output.

Thumbnails

Menu: View→Thumbnails

Both: Shift+F6

Thumbnails mode is primarily useful when dragging whole pages around within a document, or from one document to another.

Show/Hide Guides

Menu: View→Show/Hide Guides

Both: F7

I use this one about a million times each day.

Snap to Guides

Menu: View→Snap to Guides

Both: Shift+F7

If you want to drag something close to a guide but not have it snap to that guide, use this to turn off the snapping action.

Menus

Show/Hide Baseline Grid

Menu: View→Show/Hide Baseline Grid

Mac: Option+F7

Windows: Ctrl+F7

You can set up your document's baseline grid in the Preferences dialog box. Usually, the grid is based on the leading of your body text.

Show/Hide Rulers

Menu: View→Show/Hide Rulers

Mac: Cmd+R

Windows: Ctrl+R

Show/Hide Invisibles

Menu: View→Show/Hide Invisibles

Mac: Cmd+I

Windows: Ctrl+I

Invisibles means invisible text characters, such as tabs, spaces, returns, soft returns, and so on. I like working with Invisibles turned on much of the time, but it's annoying to many people.

Tile Documents As Thumbnails

Mac: Option+Tile

Windows: Alt+Tile

When you hold down Option/Alt and then select Tile from the Windows menu (on the Macintosh, the Window submenu is under the View menu), XPress automatically changes all the documents to Thumbnails view at the same time. This is great when you need to drag one or more pages from one document to another.

Note that this also works with the Stack Documents feature, although I can't think of why you'd want to use that.

Menus

Utilities Menu

The Utilities menu is a catch-all filled with features that don't really fit anyplace else. The features added by commercial XTensions can often be found here.

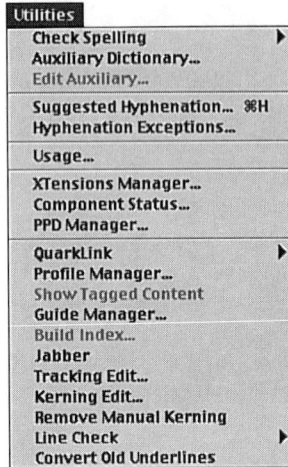

```
Utilities
  Check Spelling                    ▶
  Auxiliary Dictionary...
  Edit Auxiliary...

  Suggested Hyphenation...  ⌘H
  Hyphenation Exceptions...

  Usage...

  XTensions Manager...
  Component Status...
  PPD Manager...

  QuarkLink                         ▶
  Profile Manager...
  Show Tagged Content
  Guide Manager...
  Build Index...
  Jabber
  Tracking Edit...
  Kerning Edit...
  Remove Manual Kerning
  Line Check                        ▶
  Convert Old Underlines
```

Check Spelling: Word

Menu: Utilities→Check Spelling→Word

Mac: Cmd+L

Windows: Ctrl+W

You don't have to select the whole word; just put the cursor anywhere in it. If you have more than one word selected, this changes to Check Selection.

Check Spelling: Story

Menu: Utilities→Check Spelling→Story

Mac: Cmd+Option+L

Windows: Ctrl+Alt+W

This feature checks the spelling of the currently selected text box and all other boxes that are linked to it. It won't check the spelling of other text boxes in your document.

Check Spelling: Document

Menu: Utilities→Check Spelling→Document

Mac: Cmd+Option+Shift+L

Windows: Ctrl+Alt+Shift+W

When you're on a master page, this checks the spelling on all your master pages.

Skip Word (in Spelling)

Mac: Cmd+S

Windows: Alt+S

Of course, Cmd+S on the Macintosh is usually Save, but when the Spelling dialog box is open, it means skip the word.

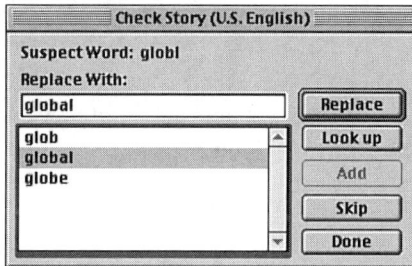

Check Story (U.S. English)
Suspect Word: globl
Replace With:
global   Replace
glob   Look up
global   Add
globe   Skip
Done

Lookup Word (in Spelling)

Mac: Cmd+L

Windows: Alt+L

Done (in Spelling)

Both: Esc

Menus

Add Word (in Spelling)

Mac: Cmd+A

Windows: Alt+A

This adds a word to your auxiliary dictionary. Of course, it only
works if you have first specified an auxiliary dictionary for your
document by selecting Auxiliary Dictionary from the Utility
menu. If you use the Auxiliary Dictionary feature while no documents are open, XPress will apply your dictionary to every new
document you create.

Add All Suspect Words to Auxiliary Dictionary

Mac: Option+Shift+Done

Windows: Alt+Shift+Close

This is one of my favorite hidden tricks: If you have a bunch of
words that you want to add to your auxiliary dictionary, type them
all in a text box and then select Check Spelling→Story. When the
Check Spelling dialog box appears, hold down Option/Alt and
then click the Done or Close button.

Suggested Hyphenation

Menu: Utilities→Suggested Hyphenation

Mac: Cmd+H

Windows: Ctrl+H

This is a very simple feature. It simply tells you how XPress thinks
a word should be hyphenated.

Font Usage

Menu: Utilities→Usage

Mac: F13 or Cmd+F6

Windows: F2

The Cmd+F6 shortcut was added at the last minute to QuarkXPress 5. This was so that users with Macintosh Powerbooks could have a keyboard shortcut because the function keys on the laptops only reach to F12.

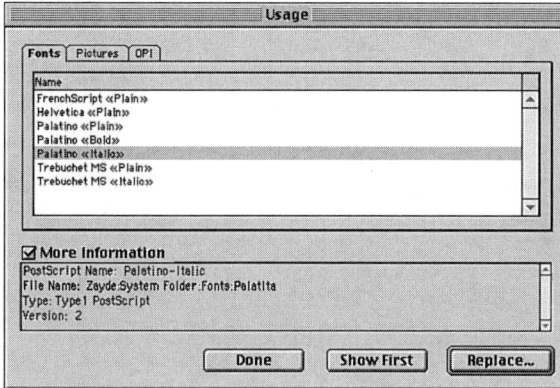

Picture Usage

Menu: Utilities→Usage

Mac: Option+F13 or Cmd+Option+F6

Windows: Shift+F2

The Cmd+Option+F6 shortcut was added at the last minute to QuarkXPress 5. This is so that users with Macintosh Powerbooks could have a keyboard shortcut because the function keys on the laptops only reach to F12.

Moving

Scrolling

Using the scroll bars to move around your document can be a real hassle if you're trying to move quickly. Here are a few shortcuts to get you where you want to go quicker.

Scroll Up One Screen

Mac: Page Up or Ctrl+K

Windows: Page Up

Scroll Down One Screen

Mac: Page Down or Ctrl+L

Windows: Page Down

Scroll with Grabber Hand

Mac: Option+drag

Windows: Alt+drag

The Grabber Hand is the best tool for moving around your page. I use this keyboard shortcut more than almost any other.

Live Scroll Toggle

Mac: Option+drag Scroll Box

Windows: Alt+drag Scroll Box

When you drag that little rectangle in the scroll bars you usually don't see your page move. However, hold down Option or Alt when you drag, and you can see the document scroll by. If you find yourself doing this a lot, open Edit→Preferences and turn on the Live Scroll checkbox. Now holding down the modifier key turns *off* Live Scroll instead of turning it on.

Moving Selected Items

When the Item tool is selected, the following keyboard shortcuts apply to moving objects (text boxes, picture boxes, lines, and so on). When the Content tool is selected, the shortcuts move pictures inside picture boxes. When one or more points on a Bézier path are selected, these shortcuts move just the selected points.

Nudge an Object in One-Point Increments

Both: Arrow keys

Nudge an Object in 1/10-Point Increments

Mac: Option+Arrow keys

Windows: Alt+Arrow keys

Move an Object with Horizontal and Vertical Constraint

Both: Shift+drag

Note that you have to start dragging and *then* hold down the Shift key because Shift-clicking on the object itself can deselect it!

Zooming and Magnification

Toggle 100%/Fit in Window (When Caps Lock Is On)

Mac: Option+click

Note that this only works in QuarkXPress 4, and as of this writing won't work in version 5. When Caps Lock key is not turned on, this keystroke gives you the Grabber Hand.

Toggle 100%/200% View

Mac: Cmd+Option+click

Windows: Ctrl+Alt+click

Zoom In

Mac: Ctrl+Shift+click or Ctrl+Shift+drag

Windows: Ctrl+Spacebar+click or Ctrl+Spacebar+drag

This is great when you want to zoom in on a particular area of your page. If you want, you can watch the View percentage in the lower left corner of the document window while you drag, and it'll show you what zoom percentage you'll get when you let go of the mouse button.

QuarkXPress usually zooms in, or out with the next keystroke, by 25 percent each time you click. If you want to change this, double-click on the Zoom tool in the Tool palette. This opens the Tool Preferences dialog box. Click the Modify button, and change the Increment field to whatever you want.

Zoom Out

Mac: Ctrl+Option+click or Ctrl+Option+drag

Windows: Ctrl+Alt+spacebar-click

Fit in Window

Menu: View→Fit in Window

Mac: Cmd+Zero

Windows: Ctrl+Zero

Actual Size

Menu: View→Actual Size

Mac: Cmd+1

Windows: Ctrl+1

Moving

Custom Magnification

Mac: Ctrl+V

Windows: Ctrl+Alt+V

Use this when you know exactly what zoom percentage you want. This keystroke jumps you into the View Percentage field in the lower left corner of the document window.

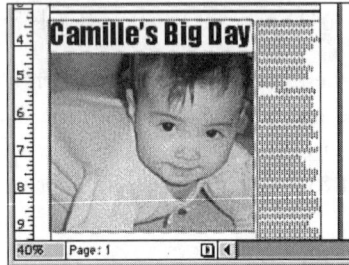

Text

Moving Through Text

If you hold down the Shift key while using the keystrokes in this section, you select from the current cursor location to where the keystroke takes you. For example, Shift+Cmd+Up Arrow (Mac) or Shift+Ctrl+Up Arrow (Windows) selects from the current cursor location to the beginning of the paragraph. Hit it again, and you add the previous paragraph to the selection.

Character by Character

Both: Left/Right Arrows

Line by Line

Both: Up/Down Arrow

Word by Word

Mac: Cmd+Left/Right Arrow

Windows: Ctrl+Left/Right Arrow

On the Macintosh, you can also move to the right one word by pressing Ctrl+] (right square bracket) and to the left with Ctrl+\ (backslash). I have no idea why they added these, as they're non-intuitive. Perhaps they're useful if the arrow keys on your keyboard break.

Next Paragraph

Mac: Cmd+Up/Down Arrow or Ctrl+hyphen

Windows: Ctrl+Up/Down Arrow

Previous Paragraph

Mac: Cmd+Up/Down Arrow

Windows: Ctrl+Up/Down Arrow

Start of Line

Mac: Cmd+Option+Left Arrow

Windows: Ctrl+Alt+Left Arrow or Home

End of Line

Mac: Cmd+Option+Right Arrow or Ctrl+Option+]

Windows: Ctrl+Alt+Right Arrow or End

Start of Story

Mac: Cmd+Option+Up Arrow

Windows: Ctrl+Alt+Up Arrow or Ctrl+Home

This is my favorite way to jump to the beginning of a story when I don't know the page on which the story begins.

End of Story

Mac: Cmd+Option+Down Arrow or Ctrl+Option+hyphen

Windows: Ctrl+Alt+Down Arrow or Ctrl+End

Here's a less-than-obvious use for this keystroke: When you have more text than will fit in a text box, you get the little red overset icon, right? If you place the cursor after the last character in the text box and then press the above keystroke with the Shift key held down, XPress selects all the overset text, even though you can't see it. Now you can use Cut or Delete or whatever you want to do with it.

Find Next Check Story Infraction

Mac: Cmd+; (semicolon)

Windows: Ctrl+;

Check Story appears only in the Utilities menu when you have the TypeTricks XTension properly installed. The tool is very useful because it lets you search for overset text boxes, orphans, widows, and other text problems.

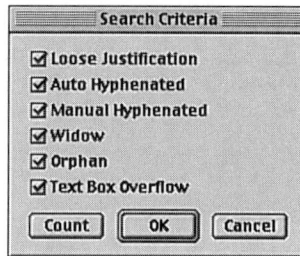

```
╔══════════ Search Criteria ══════════╗
║                                      ║
║  ☑ Loose Justification               ║
║  ☑ Auto Hyphenated                   ║
║  ☑ Manual Hyphenated                 ║
║  ☑ Widow                             ║
║  ☑ Orphan                            ║
║  ☑ Text Box Overflow                 ║
║                                      ║
║  [ Count ]  [  OK  ]  [ Cancel ]     ║
╚══════════════════════════════════════╝
```

Jump to Next Table Cell

Mac: Ctrl+Tab

Windows: Ctrl+Tab

In some programs, such as Microsoft Word, you can just press Tab to jump from one table cell to the next. Not so here, where you have to add a modifier key.

Jump to Previous Table Cell

Mac: Ctrl+Shift+Tab

Windows: Ctrl+Shift+Tab

Text

Selecting Text

One Word

Both: Double-click in word

Double-clicking on a word will not select any punctuation after that word, hence the need for the following shortcut.

One Word and Punctuation

Both: Double-click between word and punctuation

You can also double-click on the punctuation character itself.

One Line

Both: Click three times

Note that this is a single line, not a single sentence. There is no way to select a sentence automatically.

One Paragraph

Both: Click four times

Entire Story

Mac: Click five times or Cmd+A

Windows: Click five times or Ctrl+A

Drag-and-Drop Text (or Copy Text)

Mac: Cmd+Ctrl+drag or Cmd+Shift+Ctrl+drag

Some folks turn on the Drag and Drop Text option in the Preferences dialog box (Edit→Preferences), which lets them drag selected text from one place in a story to another. However, I find that I mess up my text too often when this feature is on because I'm forever dragging text when I didn't mean to. This shortcut lets me leave that feature off, and drag and drop text *only* when I really want.

Deleting Text

Delete Previous Character

Both: Delete (Backspace key)

Mac: Ctrl+H

Of course, this also deletes selected characters.

Delete Next Character

Both: ⌦ or Shift+⌦

Mac: Ctrl+Shift+H

Of course, some keyboards don't have the ⌦ key, so I just rely on Shift-Delete.

Delete Previous Word

Mac: Cmd+⌦

Windows: Ctrl+Backspace

Delete Next Word

Mac: Cmd+⌦ or Cmd+Shift+⌦

Windows: Ctrl+Delete or Ctrl+Shift+Backspace

Text

Text

Character Formats

Character Format

Menu: Style→Character

Mac: Cmd+Shift+D

Windows: Ctrl+Shift+D

Character Attributes in
the Windows version

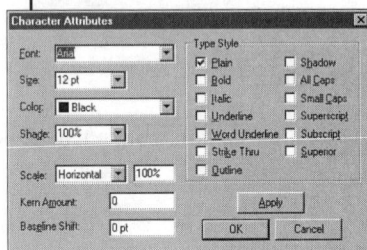

Increase Point Size (Presets)

Mac: Cmd+Shift+. (period key)

Windows: Ctrl+Shift+. (period key)

This jumps to the next built-in size presets: 7, 9, 10, 12, 14, 18, 24, 36, 48, 60, 72, 96, 122, 144, 168, 192.

Decrease Point Size (Presets)

Mac: Cmd+Shift+, (comma key)

Windows: Ctrl+Shift+, (comma key)

Increase Point Size One Point

Mac: Cmd+Shift+Option+.

Windows: Ctrl+Alt+Shift+. (period key)

This and the next shortcut are much more useful when fine-tuning the size of type.

Decrease Point Size One Point

Mac: Cmd+Shift+Option+,

Windows: Ctrl+Alt+Shift+, (comma key)

Other Size

Menu: Style→Size→Other

Mac: Cmd+Shift+\ (backslash)

Windows: Ctrl+Shift+\ (backslash)

This simply opens the Character Attributes dialog box, and selects the Size field, but it's good when you want to be specific about size.

Plain Text

Menu: Style→Type Style→Plain

Mac: Cmd+Shift+P

Windows: Ctrl+Shift+P

Plain text just means the font without any formatting—no bold, italic, superscript, and so on.

Bold

Menu: Style→Type Style→Bold

Mac: Cmd+Shift+B

Windows: Ctrl+Shift+B

The shortcut for Bold (as well as the other styles in this section, such as Italic, Underline, and so on) toggles the style on and then off again.

Italic

Menu:	Style→Type Style→Italic
Mac:	Cmd+Shift+I
Windows:	Ctrl+Shift+I

Underline

Menu:	Style→Type Style→Underline
Mac:	Cmd+Shift+U
Windows:	Ctrl+Shift+U

Word Underline

Menu:	Style→Type Style→Word Underline
Mac:	Cmd+Shift+W
Windows:	Ctrl+Shift+W

Strikethrough

Menu:	Style→Type Style→Strikethrough
Mac:	Cmd+Shift+/ (slash)
Windows:	Ctrl+Shift+/ (slash)

Outline

Menu:	Style→Type Style→Outline
Mac:	Cmd+Shift+O
Windows:	Ctrl+Shift+O

I can't really recommend using this style. It's much better to convert the text to outline (with Style→Text to Outline) and then
apply a frame.

Text

Shadow

Menu: Style→Type Style→Shadow

Mac: Cmd+Shift+S

Windows: Ctrl+Shift+S

This creates the world's ugliest shadow effect. Ignore this shortcut. If you really want good shadows, check out a commercial
XTension such as Shadowcaster, from a lowly apprentice produc-
tion (www.alap.com).

All Caps

Menu: Style→Type Style→All Caps

Mac: Cmd+Shift+K

Windows: Ctrl+Shift+K

Small Caps

Menu: Style→Type Style→Small Caps

Mac: Cmd+Shift+H

Windows: Ctrl+Shift+H

Note that this doesn't actually apply a true small cap, such as
those in many OpenType or Expert fonts. Instead, QuarkXPress
fakes a small cap style by scaling the characters based on percent-
ages in the Preferences dialog box (Edit→Preferences).

Superscript

Menu: Style→Type Style→Superscript

Mac: Cmd+Shift+=

Windows: Ctrl+Shift+Zero

Text

Subscript

Menu:	Style→Type Style→Subscript
Mac:	Cmd+Shift+hyphen
Windows:	Ctrl+Shift+9

Superior

Menu:	Style→Type Style→Superior
Mac:	Cmd+Shift+V
Windows:	Ctrl+Shift+V

You can set the size and positioning of the Superior style in the Preferences dialog box (Edit→Preferences).

Increase Horizontal/Vertical Scaling Five Percent

Mac:	Cmd+]
Windows:	Ctrl+]

These keystrokes scale in the direction (horizontal or vertical) that you last selected from the dialog box.

Decrease Horizontal/Vertical Scaling Five Percent

Mac:	Cmd+[
Windows:	Ctrl+[

These keystrokes scale in the direction (horizontal or vertical) that you last selected from the dialog box.

Increase Horizontal/Vertical Scaling One Percent

Mac:	Cmd+Option+]
Windows:	Ctrl+Alt+]

These keystrokes scale in the direction (horizontal or vertical) that you last selected from the dialog box.

Decrease Horizontal/Vertical Scaling One Percent

Mac: Cmd+Option+[

Windows: Ctrl+Alt+[

These keystrokes scale in the direction (horizontal or vertical) that you last selected from the dialog box.

Increase Kern/Track 10 Units

Mac: Cmd+Shift+]

Windows: Ctrl+Shift+]

In their infinite wisdom, Quark set the keystrokes for Increase Wordspacing (see "Increase Wordspacing One Unit" later in this section) to the same keystroke as this on Windows. However, this is only an issue if you have the Type Tricks XTension loaded.

One unit equals 1/200 of an em space.

Decrease Kern/Track 10 Units

Mac: Cmd+Shift+[

Windows: Ctrl+Shift+[

In their infinite wisdom, Quark set the keystrokes for Decrease Wordspacing (see "Decrease Wordspacing One Unit" later in this section) to the same keystroke as this on Windows. However, this is only an issue if you have the Type Tricks XTension loaded.

Increase Kern/Track One Unit

Mac: Cmd+Option+Shift+]

Windows: Ctrl+Alt+Shift+]

Decrease Kern/Track One Unit

Mac: Cmd+Option+Shift+[

Windows: Ctrl+Alt+Shift+[

Text

Increase Wordspacing One Unit (with Type Tricks XTension)

Mac: Cmd+Option+Shift+Ctrl+]

Windows: Ctrl+Shift+]

When you change the wordspacing, XPress performs kerning between each space character in the selected text and the following character.

Unfortunately on Windows, this is the same keystroke for Increase Kern/Track 10 Units, but only when the Type Tricks XTension is loaded.

Decrease Wordspacing One Unit (with Type Tricks XTension)

Mac: Cmd+Option+Shift+Ctrl+[

Windows: Ctrl+Shift+[

When you change the wordspacing, XPress performs kerning between each space character in the selected text and the following character.

Unfortunately on Windows, this is the same keystroke for Increase Kern/Track 10 Units, but only when the Type Tricks XTension is loaded.

Baseline Shift Down One Point

Mac: Cmd+Option+Shift+hyphen

Windows: Ctrl+Alt+Shift+Zero

Baseline Shift Up One Point

Mac: Cmd+Option+Shift+=

Windows: Ctrl+Alt+Shift+9

Convert Text to Outline

Menu: Style→Text to Box

When you hold down the Option (Macintosh) or Alt (Windows) key when selecting this menu item, the text is automatically anchored in place.

Holding down Option/Alt
when you select Text to Box

Paragraph Formats

Paragraph Format

Menu: Style→Formats

Mac: Cmd+Shift+F

Windows: Ctrl+Shift+F

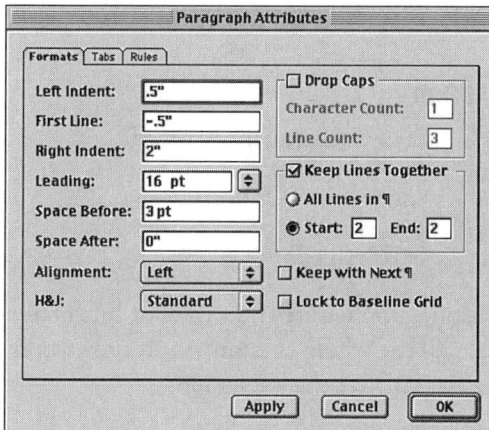

Text

Left Alignment

Menu: Style→Alignment→Left

Mac: Cmd+Shift+L

Windows: Ctrl+Shift+L

Right Alignment

Menu: Style→Alignment→Right

Mac: Cmd+Shift+R

Windows: Ctrl+Shift+R

Center Alignment

Menu: Style→Alignment→Center

Mac: Cmd+Shift+C

Windows: Ctrl+Shift+C

Justified Alignment

Menu: Style→Alignment→Justified

Mac: Cmd+Shift+J

Windows: Ctrl+Shift+J

Forced Justification

Menu: Style→Alignment→Forced

Mac: Cmd+Shift+Option+J

Windows: Ctrl+Alt+Shift+J

Forced Justification ensures that the last line of a paragraph reaches across the whole column, but it only works if there is a carriage return after the paragraph.

Leading

Menu: Style→Leading

Mac: Cmd+Shift+E

Windows: Ctrl+Shift+E

This shortcut simply opens the Paragraph Attributes dialog box and selects the Leading field.

Tabs

Menu: Style→Tabs

Mac: Cmd+Shift+T

Windows: Ctrl+Shift+T

This shortcut opens the Paragraph Attributes dialog box, and jumps to the Tabs tab.

Rule Above and Rule Below

Menu: Style→Rules

Mac: Cmd+Shift+N

Windows: Ctrl+Shift+N

This shortcut opens the Paragraph Attributes dialog box, and jumps to the Rules tab.

Increase Leading One Point

Mac: Cmd+Shift+"

Windows: Ctrl+Shift+"

This is a fast way to switch from auto leading, which you should almost never use, to absolute leading, which specifies a particular value for leading.

Decrease Leading One Point

Mac: Cmd+Shift+;

Windows: Ctrl+Shift+;

Increase Leading 1/10 Point

Mac: Cmd+Option+Shift+"

Windows: Ctrl+Alt+Shift+"

Remember that the Option/Alt key is the "make better" key! In this case, it makes the increments finer.

Decrease Leading 1/10 Point

Mac: Cmd+Option+Shift+;

Windows: Ctrl+Alt+Shift+;

Copy Paragraph Format

Mac: Option+Shift+click-any paragraph

Windows: Alt+Shift+click-any paragraph

This is a weird one, so I'd better explain it. If you want to copy the paragraph attributes from one paragraph to another, place the cursor in the paragraph(s) you want to change; then use this shortcut, and click on the formatted paragraph. QuarkXPress only copies the paragraph formatting, such as leading, drop cap, indents, and so on—it doesn't copy any of the character formatting, such as font, size, etc.

Apply No Style Before Applying Style Sheet

Mac: Option+click-on style sheet in Style Sheets palette

Windows: Alt+click-on style sheet in Style Sheets palette

When someone selects a word or paragraph and then changes its font, size, or any other attribute, that's called *local* formatting because it overrides whatever style sheet is applied to the text. This shortcut completely wipes out all the local formatting, including bold and italic styles, before it applies the style sheet.

Special Formatting Characters

One Symbol Character

Mac: Cmd+Shift+Q

Windows: Ctrl+Shift+Q

This changes only the next character to the Symbol font. I'm sure this is useful for someone, but I'm not sure whom.

One Zapf Dingbats Character

Mac: Cmd+Shift+Z

Windows: Ctrl+Shift+Z

This changes only the next character you type to the Zapf Ding-bats font, if you have it installed on your computer. I find this useful when typing special bullets. (My favorite bullet is the letter **n** in Zapf Dingbats—try it!)

Soft Return (New Line)

Mac: Shift+Return

Windows: Shift+Enter

The soft return character forces a line break, but doesn't start a new paragraph. This is extremely useful when trying to fix bad line endings.

Discretionary New Line

Mac: Cmd+Return

Windows: Ctrl+Enter

If you put a discretionary new line character in the middle of a word, it'll break at the end of the line if it needs to; but if it doesn't need to break, it'll be invisible and it won't change the formatting at all. For example, you might use it in the middle of an Internet URL address that may or may not break across lines, if you don't want it to have a hyphen.

Discretionary Hyphen

Mac: Cmd+hyphen

Windows: Ctrl+hyphen

You can put a discretionary hyphen (also called a "dischy") in the middle of a word to let XPress hyphenate that word at that location. It doesn't force XPress to hyphenate it; rather, it just allows it, if necessary. Also, if you put a dischy *before* a word, it tells XPress to *not* hyphenate it.

Nonbreaking Hyphen

Mac: Cmd+=

Windows: Ctrl+=

Don't want a hyphenated word to break from one line to the next? Use a non-breaking hyphen instead. It's a rare occasion, but it can be useful.

Nonbreaking Space

Mac: Cmd+Space or Ctrl+Space

Windows: Ctrl+5

The nonbreaking space keeps words together so they won't break at the end of a line.

Next Column

Mac: Enter or Ctrl+C

Windows: Enter on keypad

If you need to force the text to jump to the next column, this is the shortcut for you.

Next Text Box

Mac: Shift+Enter or Ctrl+Shift+C

Windows: Shift+Enter on keypad

En Space

Mac: Option+Space

Windows: Ctrl+Shift+6

An en space is one-half an em space. By default, an en space is the width of the character 0 (zero) in whatever font and size you're working with. However, if you turn on the Standard Em Space option in the Preferences dialog box, an en space is exactly one-half the width of the size of your text. That is, in 14-point text, an en space would be 7 points wide.

Nonbreaking En Space

Mac: Cmd+Option+Space or Cmd+Option+5

Windows: Ctrl+Alt+Shift+6

Flex Space

Mac: Option+Shift+Space

Windows: Ctrl+Shift+5

They call it the Flex Space because it can be any size you want. The default is half an en space, but you can change it in the Preferences dialog box.

Nonbreaking Flex Space

Mac: Cmd+Option+Shift+Space

Windows: Ctrl+Alt+Shift+5

Punctuation Space

Both: Shift+Space

Nonbreaking Punctuation Space

Mac: Cmd+Shift+Space

Windows: Ctrl+Shift+Space

Nonbreaking En Dash

Windows: Ctrl+Alt+Shift+hyphen

On the Macintosh, en dashes are always nonbreaking.

Breaking Em Dash

Mac: Option+Shift+hyphen

Windows: Ctrl+Shift+=

Nonbreaking Em Dash

Mac: Cmd+Option+=

Windows: Ctrl+Alt+Shift+=

Current Page Number

Mac: Cmd+3

Windows: Ctrl+3

This is the key to making automatic page numbers in XPress: Put the current page number character on a master page.

Previous Text Box Page Number

Mac: Cmd+2

Windows: Ctrl+2

Next Text Box Page Number

Mac: Cmd+4

Windows: Ctrl+4

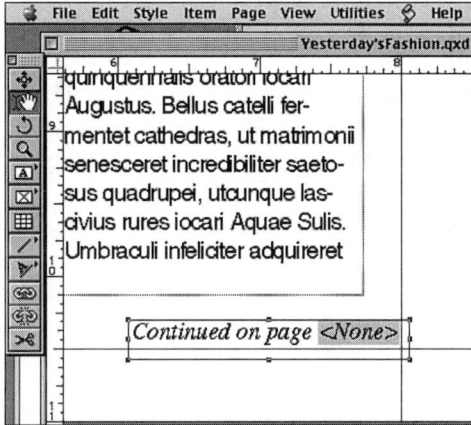

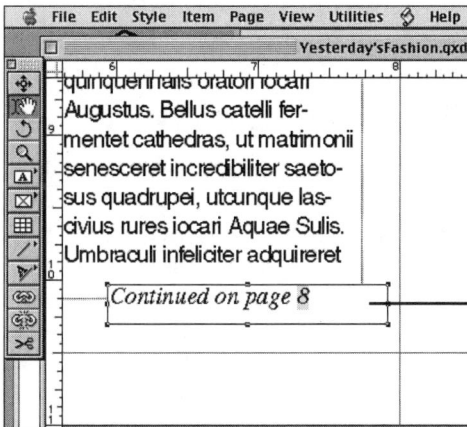

When the text box overlaps, the page number updates.

Indent to Here

Mac: Cmd+ \ (backslash)

Windows: Ctrl+ \ (backslash)

This character forces the rest of the paragraph to indent to that point.
If you put it after a bullet, the bullet will appear to hang out in the
left margin. Similarly, you can make a quotation mark hang out, such
as in a pull quote, by placing this character after the quotation mark.

Flush Right Tab

Mac: Option+Tab

Windows: Shift+Tab

There are two problems with putting a tab stop at the right margin. First, it's hard to place it exactly in the right spot. Second, if the indents or text box width changes, the tab settings are all messed up. This shortcut adds a tab that always aligns with the right indent, no matter what the indent setting or text box width.

Smart Quotes Toggle

Both: Control-quote or Control-Shift-quote

This is a toggle because it depends on whether Smart Quotes is turned on or off in the Preferences dialog box. If Smart Quotes is turned on, this shortcut will give you a straight quote. If that preference is turned off, this will give you a curly quote.

Find/Change Characters

It's easy to search for the letter Q and replace it with the letter B, although I have no idea why you'd want to. However, it's less obvious how to search for or replace with invisible characters like tabs. The trick is to use the codes or keyboard shortcuts in the Find/Change palette.

Another way to type these codes into the Find/Change palette is to select the character you want in a text box, copy it, and then paste it in the Find or Change field.

Tab

Mac: \t or Cmd+Tab

Windows: \t or Ctrl+Tab

New Paragraph

Mac: \p or Cmd+Return

Windows: \p or Ctrl+Enter

New Line

Mac: \n or Cmd+Shift+Return

Windows: \n or Ctrl+Shift+Enter

New Column

Mac: \c or Cmd+Enter

Windows: \c or Ctrl+Enter

New Box

Mac: \b or Cmd+Shift+Enter

Windows: \b or Ctrl+Shift+Enter

Previous Text Box Page Number

Mac: \2 or Cmd+2

Windows: \2 or Ctrl+2

Current Page Number

Mac: \3 or Cmd+3

Windows: \3 or Ctrl+3

Next Text Box Page Number

Mac: \4 or Cmd+4

Windows: \4 or Ctrl+4

Text

Wildcard

Mac: \ ? or Cmd+?

Windows: \ ? or Ctrl+?

You can only use the wildcard character in the Find field of the Find/Change palette. For example, if you type **d\?g** in the Find field, XPress will find dog, dig, dug, and so on.

Punctuation Space

Mac: \ . or Cmd+. (period key)

Windows: \ . or Ctrl+. (period key)

Flex Space

Mac: \ f or Cmd+Shift+F

Windows: \ f or Ctrl+Shift+F

Backslash

Mac: \ \ or Cmd+\ (backslash)

Windows: \ \ or Ctrl+\ (backslash)

Because several of the codes above use the backslash character, if you want to search for or replace with the backslash character, you have to type it twice.

Pictures and Lines

Changing the Picture

Increase Size by Five Percent

Mac: Cmd+Option+Shift+. (period key)

Windows: Ctrl+Alt+Shift+. (period key)

This works when either the Item or Content tool is selected. This (and the following shortcut) only changes the size of the picture, not the picture box.

Decrease Size by Five Percent

Mac: Cmd+Option+Shift+, (comma key)

Windows: Ctrl+Alt+Shift+, (comma key)

This works when either the Item or Content tool is selected.

Center Picture in Box

Menu: Style→Center Picture

Mac: Cmd+Shift+M

Windows: Ctrl+Shift+M

While the keyboard shortcut works in any version of XPress, the menu item is new in XPress 5.

Fit Picture to Box

Menu: Style→Fit Picture to Box

Mac: Cmd+Shift+F

Windows: Ctrl+Shift+F

I almost never use this shortcut because it usually scales the picture anamorphically (different horizontal and vertical scaling). Note that while the keyboard shortcut works in any version of XPress, the menu item is new in XPress 5.

Fit Picture Maintaining Ratio

Menu: Style→Fit Picture to Box (Proportionally)

Mac: Cmd+Option+Shift+F

Windows: Ctrl+Alt+Shift+F

This is what I generally use to scale images up or down. While the keyboard shortcut works in any version of XPress, the menu item is new in XPress 5.

Move Picture One Point

Both: Arrow keys

When you have the Item tool selected, this moves the picture box. When you have the Content tool selected, this moves the picture inside the box.

Move Picture 1/10 Point

Mac: Option+Arrow keys

Windows: Alt+Arrow keys

Whether the picture box or the picture inside the box moves depends on whether you have the Item tool or the Content tool selected.

Negative

Menu:	Style→Negative
Mac:	Cmd+Shift+hyphen
Windows:	Ctrl+Shift+hyphen

Negative works best with TIFF and JPEG images, and it won't work at all with EPS images. On 1-bit (what Adobe Photoshop calls Bitmap mode) TIFF images, this inverts solid and transparent pixels. What was white becomes solid color, and what was black becomes transparent.

Halftone Specifications

Mac:	Cmd+Shift+H
Windows:	Ctrl+Shift+H

This feature is a holdover from much earlier days. I don't recommend you use it. If you want custom halftone effects, do them in Adobe Photoshop.

Contrast Specifications

Mac:	Cmd+Shift+C
Windows:	Ctrl+Shift+C

This feature is a very blunt instrument. You will always get a better result by making contrast adjustments in a program like Adobe Photoshop.

Modifying Boxes

Here are shortcuts that work for both text and picture boxes.

Resize Picture Box

Both:	Drag Handle

You can drag any corner or side handle of a box to resize it, but this won't resize the contents of the box.

Constrain to Square or Circle

Both: Shift+drag-handle

Maintain Aspect Ratio

Mac: Shift+Option+drag

Windows: Alt+Shift+drag-handle

This shortcut lets you resize the box, although not its contents, with the same height/width proportions.

Scale Picture with Box

Mac: Cmd+drag

Windows: Ctrl+drag-handle

Holding down Cmd (Mac) or Ctrl (Windows) is the key to scaling the contents along with the box.

Scale Picture and Constrain Box Shape

Mac: Cmd+Shift+drag-handle

Windows: Ctrl+Shift+drag-handle

Maintain Ratio of Box and Picture

Mac: Cmd+Shift+Option+drag

Windows: Ctrl+Shift+Alt+drag-handle

Bézier Editing

Edit Shape Toggle

Menu: Item→Edit→Shape

Mac: Shift+F4

Windows: F10

When you convert text to outlines (Style→Text to Box), you see all the points along the Bézier curves, which makes it easy to alter the text outlines but difficult to manipulate the outlined text as a whole. Use this shortcut to display the bounding box of the Bézier shape instead of the individual points.

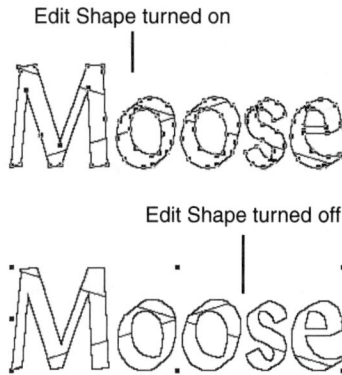

Edit Shape turned on

Edit Shape turned off

Add Point

Mac:	Option+click-segment
Windows:	Alt+click-segment

Obviously this shortcut, as well as all the others in this section, only works when Edit Shape is turned on. A segment is the part of the line between two points.

Delete Bézier Point

Mac:	Option+click-point
Windows:	Alt+click-point or Backspace

Note that adding and removing a point use the same shortcut, though the cursor looks slightly different (a squarish circle or a circle with an X in it. Which you get depends on whether you click a segment or a point.

Delete Active Point While Drawing

Mac: Delete

Windows: Backspace

This is helpful when you click someplace accidentally. Press Delete or Backspace and that point disappears.

Change to Smooth Point

Menu: Item→Point/Segment Type→Smooth Point

Mac: Ctrl+drag or Option+F2

Windows: Ctrl+Shift+drag-handle or Ctrl+F2

Of course, you have to have one or more points selected to use this or any of the following shortcuts. After selecting the path, click again on a point to select it. You can also select more than one point by Shift-clicking on each additional point.

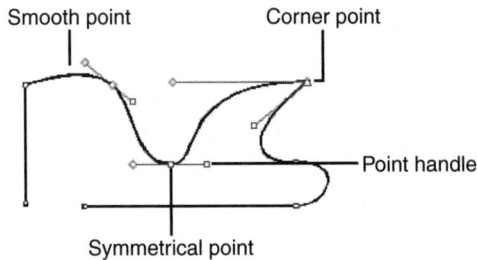

Smooth point   Corner point   Point handle   Symmetrical point

Change to Corner Point

Menu: Item→Point/Segment Type→Corner Point

Mac: Ctrl+click or Ctrl+drag on handle or Option+F2

Windows: Ctrl+Shift+drag-handle or Ctrl+F1

Change to Symmetrical Point

Menu: Item→Point/Segment Type→Symmetrical Point

Mac: Option+F3

Windows: Ctrl+F3

Change to Straight Segment

Menu: Item→Point/Segment Type→Straight Segment

Mac: Option+Shift+F1

Windows: Ctrl+Shift+F1

To change a segment, you have to have two or more adjacent points on the path selected. You can select two or more adjacent points quickly by clicking on the segment between the points. However, if you want to select more than one segment at a time, you have to select the points individually.

Change to Curved Segment

Menu: Item→Point/Segment Type→Curved Segment

Mac: Option+Shift+F2

Windows: Ctrl+Shift+F2

Change Smooth to Corner Point While Drawing

Mac: Cmd+Ctrl+drag-handle

Windows: Ctrl+F1

Edit Path While Still Drawing

Mac: Cmd+drag

Windows: Ctrl+drag

Many people don't realize that you can edit any point along a curve, or any handle coming off a curve point while you're still drawing. As long as you don't deselect the path accidentally, you can go back to drawing the path after making your edits.

Retract Curve Handles

Mac: Ctrl+Option+click-point

Windows: Ctrl+Shift+click-point

This simply removes the handles.

Expose Curve Handles

Mac: Ctrl+Option+drag-point

Windows: Ctrl+Shift+drag-point

When you retract the curve handles with the previous shortcut, you can drag out the handles again with this shortcut. If you use this on a corner point, XPress automatically converts the point into a smooth point.

Select All Points in Active Box

Mac: Cmd+Shift+A or double-click edge of box

Windows: Ctrl+Shift+A or double-click edge of box

If your object is made up of more than one path, such as text converted to outlines, double-clicking on the edge of the box only selects one path among all of them. To get all the paths, you should triple-click.

Select All Points in Active Path

Mac: Cmd+Shift+A

Windows: Ctrl+Shift+A

Both: Double-click point or double-click path

Remember that in QuarkXPress, *paths* are always open and *boxes* are always closed objects.

Constrain Active Point/Handle to 45 Degree Movement

Both: Shift+drag-point/handle

Importing Pictures

In the following shortcuts, the word Open refers to clicking the Open button in the Get Picture dialog box.

Get Picture

Mac: Cmd+E

Windows: Ctrl+E

Low-Resolution Screen Image

Both: Shift+Open

By default, TIFF images are imported with a 72-dpi screen resolution. This does not affect printing; it does affect how it appears onscreen. This shortcut gives you a 36-dpi image instead, which might speed up screen redraw of the picture on some old computers. I doubt the lower quality is worth it.

Import Line Art TIFF As Grayscale

Mac: Option+Open

Windows: Ctrl+Open

I have no idea why you would want to convert a line art TIFF into a grayscale TIFF. Each pixel is still either black or white, so it makes no sense. Oh well.

TIFF Grayscale to Line Art

Mac: Cmd+Open

Windows: Ctrl+Open

This forces grayscale TIFF images into line art images (what Adobe Photoshop would call Bitmap), where every pixel is either black or white. You can get some interesting special effects with this.

TIFF Color to Grayscale

Mac: Cmd+Open

Windows: Ctrl+Open

There's no doubt that you'll get a better conversion from color to grayscale in Adobe Photoshop, but if you're in a hurry, it's nice to know you can do it here. Note that this won't affect the image on disk—it only changes how it appears onscreen and how it prints.

Don't Import Spot Colors in EPS

Mac: Cmd+Open

Windows: Ctrl+Open

This is more or less the same thing as importing an EPS that contains a spot color; then going to the Edit Colors dialog box (Edit→Colors) and deleting that spot color. This forces the spot color to separate as a process color. However, here's a tip: If you're trying to get your spot colors to print as process colors, either edit the color by turning off the Spot Color check box (in the Edit Colors dialog box), or change the settings in the Output tab of the Print dialog box to Process Only. Both of these are more flexible than this shortcut.

Force Reimport of All Pictures

Mac: Cmd+Open

Windows: Ctrl+Open

In this case, "Open" refers to the Open button in the Open dialog box. In XPress 4, this is really handy when you need to update dozens (or hundreds) of pictures that are all modified. In XPress 5, it's less useful because of the next shortcut.

Update All Pictures

Mac: Option+Update

Windows: Alt+Update

Updating a number of modified pictures in the Picture Usage dialog box (Utilities→Usage) has always been a hassle because you have to confirm each and every image, one at a time. Fortunately, Quark snuck this little efficiency shortcut into XPress 5 before it shipped (I don't think it's even in the manuals), which bypasses all the **Are you sure?** alerts.

Lines

Increase Width (Presets)

Mac: Cmd+Shift+. (period key)

Windows: Ctrl+Shift+. (period key)

Note that these (and the following four shortcuts) are the same shortcuts as increasing the size of text.

Decrease Width (Presets)

Mac: Cmd+Shift+, (comma key)

Windows: Ctrl+Shift+, (comma key)

Increase Width One Point

Mac: Cmd+Option+Shift+. (period key)

Windows: Ctrl+Alt+Shift+. (period key)

Decrease Width One Point

Mac: Cmd+Option+Shift+, (comma key)

Windows: Ctrl+Alt+Shift+, (comma key)

Pictures and Lines

Other Width

Mac: Cmd+\ (backslash)

Windows: Ctrl+Shift+\ (backslash)

Constrain Resizing or Moving to 45 or 90 Degrees

Both: Shift+drag endpoint

Constrain Resizing to Angle

Mac: Shift+Option+drag endpoint

Windows: Shift+Alt+drag endpoint

This lets you make a straight line longer or shorter while retaining its angle while having no effect on Bézier curves. It's the same shortcut as maintaining the height and width of a box while dragging.

Easter Eggs

Hidden Featurettes

It's a tradition for software engineers to include hidden features in their programs. Sometimes they are actually useful, but usually they're Easter eggs—useless features that are just plain fun.

Super Delete

Mac: Cmd+Option+Shift+K (Marvin)

Windows: Ctrl+Alt+Shift+K (Meltdown)

When Quark first included Marvin the Martian and Meltdown Easter eggs back in QuarkXPress 3.2, many users thought their computers had been infected with some sort of weird virus. Fortunately, they're just a fun diversion to make you smile. On the other hand, if you have no sense of humor, I suggest simply not pressing these keystrokes.

Who's Who at Quark

Mac: Cmd+Option+Shift+click

Windows: Caps Lock+Ctrl+Shift+click

To see these fun pictures of Quark employees, you have to open the Environments dialog box first by pressing Option+Help (Mac), Cmd+Option+Ctrl+E (Mac), or hold down the Ctrl key while selecting About QuarkXPress from the Help menu (Windows); then click (with the modifier keys listed above) on that dialog box. Note that the who's who pictures change between one version of XPress and the next.

Taste the Rainbow

Both: Create a new dash using Edit→Dashes and Stripes named *taste the rainbow*.

This is one of my favorite practical jokes to play on an unsuspecting XPress user. After you create a new dash called **taste the rainbow**, every dialog box that shows a list of items such as the Edit Colors and the Edit Dashes and Stripes dialog boxes become colorized. You have to see it to believe it.

Even better, after you turn on this effect, select any text box with the Content tool and then Cmd+Shift+Option+click (Mac) or Ctrl+Alt+Shift+right-click (Windows) on any style sheet in the Style Sheets palette. I'm not even going to tell you what happens!

Unfortunately, just before version 5.0 shipped, Quark pulled this Easter egg out. With luck, they'll sneak it back into the next revision.

Easter Eggs

Function Keys

If the function keys don't work for you and you're working on a Macintosh, the operating system has probably grabbed all your function keys. Here's what you do: Select Apple Menu, Control Panels, Keyboard; then click the Function Keys button and turn off the Enable Hot Function Keys check box. Now, your QuarkXPress function keys will probably work again.

On the other hand, there is a somewhat obscure problem with some versions of the Keyboard control panel and some Macintosh computers that stops the function keys from operating properly when the Option key is held down. If you run into this, and if you're not working with multiple keyboard layouts (most people don't), it's safe to disable the Keyboard control panel with the Extensions Manager. That should fix it. If you do need the Keyboard control panel, you can try using an earlier version of the control panel, which you can find on an earlier system install disk.

Function Key	Macintosh	Windows
F1	Undo	Help
Shift+F1		Contextual help
Option+F1	Change to corner point	
Option+Shift+F1	Change to line segment	
Ctrl+F1		Change to corner point
Ctrl+Shift+F1		Change to line segment
F2	Cut	Font Usage
Shift+F2		Picture Usage
Option+F2	Change to smooth point	
Option+Shift+F2	Change to curved segment	
Ctrl+F2		Change to smooth point
Ctrl+Shift+F2		Change to curved segment
F3	Copy	Maximize window
Shift+F2		Fit Spread
Option+F3	Change to symmetrical point	
Ctrl+F3		Change to symmetrical point
Ctrl+Shift+F3		Previous master page
F4	Paste	Show/Hide Document Layout
Shift+F4	Edit Shape	Toggle between master pages and document pages
Option+F4	Edit Runaround shape [1]	

Function Key	Macintosh	Windows
Option+Shift+F4	Edit clipping path shape	
Ctrl+F4		Close
Ctrl+Shift+F4		Next master page
F5	Bring to Front	Bring to Front
Shift+F5	Send to Back	Send to Back
Option+F5	Bring Forward	
Shift+Option+F5	Send Backward	
Ctrl+F5		Bring Forward
Ctrl+Shift+F5		Send Backward
F6	Lock/Unlock	Lock/Unlock
Shift+F6	Thumbnails view	Thumbnails view
Cmd+F6	Font Usage	
Cmd+Option+F6	Picture Usage	
Ctrl+F6		Previous Document
Ctrl+Shift+F6		Next Document
F7	Show/Hide Guides	Show/Hide Guides
Shift+F7	Snap to Guides	Snap to Guides
Option+F7	Show/Hide Baseline Grid	
Ctrl+F7		Show/Hide Baseline Grid
F8	Show/Hide Tools	Show/Hide Tools
Shift+F8	Toggle Item/Content tool	Toggle Item/Content tool
Option+F8	Next Tool	
Shift+Option+F8	Previous Tool	
Ctrl+F8		Next Tool
Ctrl+Shift+F8		Previous Tool
F9	Show/Hide Measurements palette	Show/Hide Measurements palette
Shift+F9	Edit font name field	Edit font name field
Option+F9	Next font in list [2]	
Shift+Option+F9	Previous font in list [3]	
Ctrl+F9		Next font in list
Ctrl+Shift+F9		Previous font in list
F10	Show/Hide Document Layout palette	Edit Shape
Shift+F10	Toggle between master pages and document pages	Context (right-button) menu
Option+F10	Next master page	
Shift+Option+F10	Previous master page	

Function Key	Macintosh	Windows
Ctrl+F10		Edit Runaround
Ctrl+Shift+F10		Edit Clipping Path
F11	Show/Hide Style Sheets	Show/Hide Style Sheets
Shift+F11	Edit Style Sheets	Edit Style Sheets
Option+F11	Show/Hide Lists	
Shift+Option+F11	Edit H&Js	
Ctrl+F11		Show/Hide Lists
Ctrl+Shift+F11	Edit H&Js	
F12	Show/Hide Colors palette	Show/Hide Colors palette
Shift+F12	Edit Colors	Edit Colors
Option+F12	Show/Hide Trap Information palette	
Shift+Option+F12	Trapping Preferences	
Ctrl+F12		Show/Hide Trap Information palette
Ctrl+Shift+F12		Trapping preferences
F13	Font Usage	
Option+F13	Picture Usage	

[1] You cannot edit the shape of the runaround when the Runaround dialog box is set to Item, Same as Clipping, or Auto Image.

[2] The previous/next font is determined by font name rather than the name you see in the font list; you may not get the font you expect.

[3] The previous/next font is determined by font name rather than the name you see in the font list; you may not get the font you expect.

Context-Sensitive Menus

Sure, the Web tools are all pretty cool in QuarkXPress 5, but one of my favorite features is the lowly context-sensitive menu, which you get by holding down the right mouse button on Windows, or Ctrl+clicking on the Macintosh. The context-sensitive menu changes depending on what you click. The following lists the various context-sensitive menus, depending on what you click.

By the way, in earlier versions of QuarkXPress for Macintosh, the Ctrl key was a shortcut for the Zoom tool. In XPress 5, you can still get the Zoom tool by Ctrl+Shift+clicking. Or, if you prefer, you can reverse these shortcuts in the Interactive tab of the Preferences dialog box (Edit→Preferences). If you do, Ctrl+click gives you the Zoom tool and Ctrl+Shift+click triggers a context-sensitive menu.

Fit in Window
Actual Size
Modify...
Content ▶
Get Text...
Save Text...
Paragraph Style Sheet ▶
Character Style Sheet ▶
Send & Bring ▶
Cut
Copy
Paste
Hyperlink ▶
Anchor ▶
Add to Index
Convert Text to Table...

Text Box

Context-Sensitive
Menus

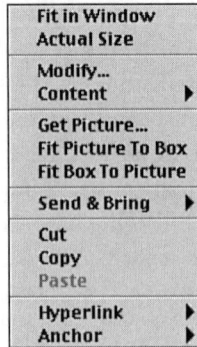

Fit in Window
Actual Size

Modify...
Content ▶

Get Picture...
Fit Picture To Box
Fit Box To Picture

Send & Bring ▶

Cut
Copy
Paste

Hyperlink ▶
Anchor ▶

Picture Box

Fit in Window
✓ Actual Size

Preferences ▶

Save
Print...
Export ▶

Cut
Copy
Paste

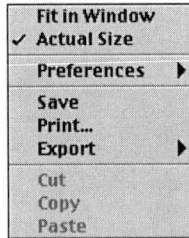

Blank part of page
or pasteboard

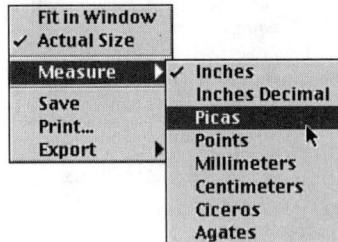

Fit in Window
✓ Actual Size

Measure ▶ | ✓ Inches
Inches Decimal
Picas
Points ▶
Millimeters
Centimeters
Ciceros
Agates

Save
Print...
Export ▶

Ruler

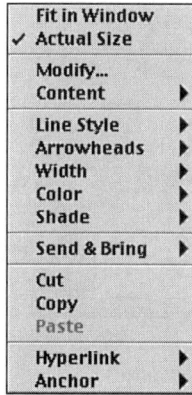

Line

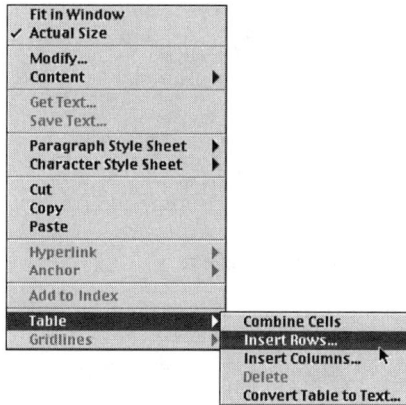

Table

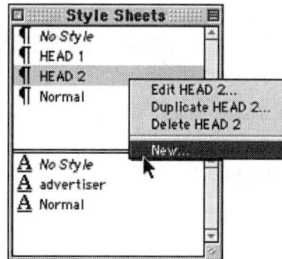

Style Sheets palette

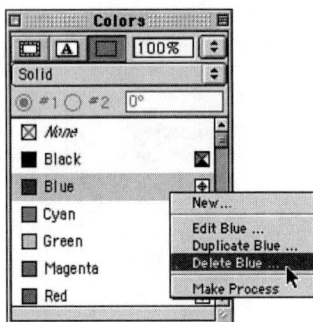

Colors palette

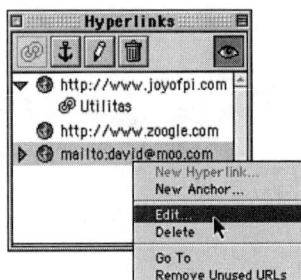

Hyperlinks palette

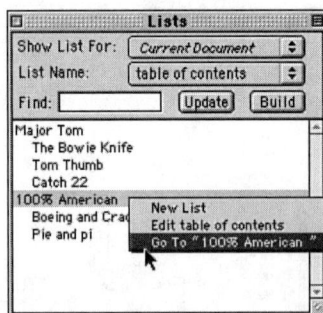

Lists palette

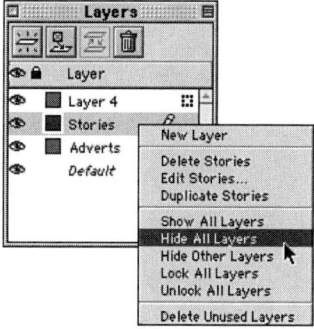

Layers palette

Special Characters

We all remember the keystrokes that we use most often, including those shortcuts for typing special characters like the em and en dashes. But how do you type the Section (§) character, or the check mark (✔) in the Zapf Dingbats font? Here's a quick-reference guide to many of the most popular characters.

For those not familiar with the Windows Alt keys, you must type them using the numeric keypad numbers while holding down the Alt key. If your PC keyboard doesn't have a numeric keypad, check to see if there is a Function key or some other method of typing numeric keypad numbers.

Name	Looks Like	Macintosh	Windows
Opening double quote	"	Option-[	Alt-0147
Closing double quote	"	Option-Shift-[	Alt-0148
Opening single quote	'	Option-]	Alt-0145
Closing single quote	'	Option-Shift-]	Alt-0146
em dash	—	Option-Shift-Hyphen	Alt-0151
en dash	–	Option-Hyphen	Alt-0150
Ellipsis	…	Option-;	Alt-0133
Fraction bar	/	Option-Shift-1	Not available
Capital ligature AE	Æ	Option-Shift-'	Alt-0198
Small ligature ae	æ	Option-'	Alt-0230
Ligature fi	fi	Option-Shift-5	Not available
Ligature fl	fl	Option-Shift-6	Not available
Bullet	•	Option-8	Shift-Alt-8 or Alt-0149
Copyright	©	Option-g	Alt-Shift-C or Alt-0169
Registered	®	Option-r	Alt-Shift-R or Alt-0174
Trademark	™	Option-2	Alt-Shift-2 or Alt-0153
Degree	°	Option-Shift-8	Alt-0176
Section	§	Option-6	Alt-Shift-6 or Alt-0167
Paragraph	¶	Option-7	Alt-Shift-7 or Alt-0182

Name	Looks Like	Macintosh	Windows
Dagger	†	Option-t	Atl-Shift-T or Alt-0134
Cents	¢	Option-4	Alt-0162
Left guillemets	«	Option-\	Alt-0171
Right guillemets	»	Option-Shift-\	Alt-0187
Left single guillemets	‹	Option-Shift-3	Alt-0139
Right single guillemets	›	Option-Shift-4	Alt-0155
Base double quote	„	Option-Shift-W	Alt-0132
Base single quote	‚	Option-Shift-0	Alt-0130
Question mark down	¿	Option-Shift-?	Alt-0191
Exclamation point down	¡	Option-1	Alt-0161
Acute vowel	áéíóúÁÉÍÓÚ	Option-E; then vowel	Alt-0225,0233,0237, 0243,0250 Alt-193,0201,0205, 0211,02180
Umlaut vowel	äëïöüÄËÏÖÜ	Option-U; then vowel	Alt-0228,0235,0239, 0246,0252 Alt-0196,0203,0207, 0214,0220
Grave vowel	àèìòùÀÈÌÒÙ	Option-~; then vowel	Alt-0224,0232,0236, 0242,0249 Alt-0192,0200,0204, 0210,0217
Circumflex vowel	âêîôûÂÊÎÔÛ	Option-I; then vowel	Alt-0226,0234,0238, 0244,0251 Alt-0194,0202,0206, 0212,0219
Cedilla C	Ç	Option-Shift-C	Alt-0199
Cedilla c	ç	Option-C	Alt-0231
Capital slashed O	Ø	Option-Shift-O	Alt-0216
Small slashed o	ø	Option-O	Alt-0248
German ess-tset (double) s	ß	Option-S	Alt-0223
Tilde	˜	Option-Shift-N	Alt-0152
Tilde N	Ñ	Option-N; then Shift-N	Alt-0209
Tilde n	ñ	Option-N; then N	Alt-0241
Circumflex	^	Option-Shift-I	Alt-0136
Macron	¯	Option-Shift-,	Not available
Breve	˘	Option-Shift-.	Not available

Name	Looks Like	Macintosh	Windows
Ring accent	°	Option-K	Alt-0176
Ring a	å	Option-A	Alt-0229
Ring A	Å	Option-Shift-A	Alt-0197
Dot accent	·	Option-H	Not available
Pound sterling	£	Option-3	Alt-0163
Yen	¥	Option-Y	Alt-0165

Zapf Dingbats Fonts

Name	Looks Like	Macintosh	Windows
Shadow ballot box up	❏	O	
Shadow ballot box down	❐	P	
3D ballot box up	❑	Q	
3D ballot box down	❒	R	
Filled ballot box	■	N	
Hollow ballot box	☐	N (apply outline style)	
Opening big quote	❝	Shift-]	
Closing big quote	❞	Option-N	Shift-` (or tilde)
Opening single big quote	❛	Shift-[	
Closing single big quote	❜	Shift-\	
Great bullet	●	L	
Great hollow bullet	○	L (apply outline style)	
Great shadow bullet	○	M	
Filled arrowhead	♠	Option-Shift-E	Alt-0228
Right arrow	→	Option-]	Alt-0220
Speeding right arrow	➠	Option-Shift-7	Alt-0224
Triangle up	▲	S	
Triangle down	▼	T	
Love leaf	❦	Option-7	Alt-0166
X-mark	✘	8	
Check-mark	✔	4	
J'accuse	☞	Shift-=	
Victory	✌	Comma	

Name	Looks Like	Macintosh	Windows
Scissors	✄	Shift-4	
Pencil straight	✐	/	
Pen nib	✑	1	
Telephone	☎	Shift-5	
Cross	✚	Shift-;	
Star	★	Shift-H	
Quatrastar	✦	Shift-F	
Octastar	✳	Shift-W	
Big asterisk	✺	Shift-Z	
Circled sun	☀	B	
Snowflake	❄	D	

The ANSI Character Set

If you use QuarkXPress for Windows, you need to know about typing ANSI characters. You can type most characters on the keyboard, but there are some characters that cannot be typed using the regular A through Z, and 0 through 9 keys. If you find a character in the following table that suits your fancy, here's how to type it. Hold down the Alt key, type a zero on the keypad (you have to have a numeric keypad to make this work), and then type the ANSI code. For example, to type Ç you would hold down the Alt key while pressing 0199. For ANSI codes 46 through 99, type two zeros before the number.

If your PC keyboard doesn't have a numeric keypad (most laptops don't), check to see if there is a Function key or some other method for typing keypad numerals.

ANSI Code	Times	Symbol	Zapf Dingbats
0–31 No characters			
32	space	space	
33	!	!	✁
34	"	∀	✂
35	#	#	✃
36	$	∃	✄
37	%	%	☎
38	&	&	✆
39	'	∋	✇
40	(	(	✈
41	)	)	✉
42	*	*	☛
43	+	+	☞
44	,	,	✌
45	-	−	✍
46	.	.	✎
47	/	/	✏
48	0	0	✐
49	1	1	✑
50	2	2	✒

ANSI Code	Times	Symbol	Zapf Dingbats
51	3	3	✓
52	4	4	✔
53	5	5	✕
54	6	6	✖
55	7	7	✗
56	8	8	✘
57	9	9	✚
58	:	:	✜
59	;	;	✛
60	<	<	✝
61	=	=	†
62	>	>	✞
63	?	?	✟
64	@	≅	✠
65	A	A	✡
66	B	B	✢
67	C	X	✣
68	D	Δ	✤
69	E	E	✥
70	F	Φ	✦
71	G	Γ	✧
72	H	H	★
73	I	I	☆
74	J	ϑ	✪
75	K	K	✫
76	L	Λ	✬
77	M	M	✭
78	N	N	✮
79	O	O	✯
80	P	Π	✰
81	Q	Θ	✱
82	R	P	✲
83	S	Σ	✳
84	T	T	✴

ANSI Code	Times	Symbol	Zapf Dingbats
85	U	Υ	✳
86	V	ς	✶
87	W	Ω	✷
88	X	Ξ	✸
89	Y	Ψ	✹
90	Z	Z	✺
91	[	[	✳
92	\	∴	✳
93	]	]	✳
94	^	⊥	✤
95	_	_	✿
96	`	‾	❁
97	a	α	❂
98	b	β	❃
99	c	χ	✻
100	d	δ	✽
101	e	ε	✾
102	f	φ	❀
103	g	γ	✵
104	h	η	✶
105	i	ι	✳
106	j	φ	✴
107	k	κ	✲
108	l	λ	●
109	m	μ	○
110	n	ν	■
111	o	o	❑
112	p	π	❐
113	q	θ	❏
114	r	ρ	❒
115	s	σ	▲
116	t	τ	▼
117	u	υ	◆
118	v	ϖ	❖

ANSI Code	Times	Symbol	Zapf Dingbats
119	w	ω	▶
120	x	ξ	I
121	y	ψ	I
122	z	ζ	∎
123	{	{	❛
124					❜
125	}	}	❝
126	~	~	❞
127 No characters			
128	€		(
129			)
130	,		(
131	ƒ		)
132	,,		(
133	…		)
134	†		❬
135	‡		❭
136	^		❨
137	‰		❩
138	Š		(
139	‹		)
140	Œ		❪
141			❫
142	Ž		
143–144 No characters			
145	'		
146	'		
147	"		
148	"		
149	•		
150	–		
151	—		
152	~		
153	™		

ANSI Code	Times	Symbol	Zapf Dingbats
154	š		
155	›		
156	œ		
157–158 No characters			
159	Ÿ		
160 No characters			
161	¡	ϒ	✁
162	¢	′	✂
163	£	≤	✃
164	¤	⁄	❤
165	¥	∞	✺
166	¦	ƒ	✿
167	§	♣	☜
168	¨	♦	♣
169	©	♥	♦
170	ª	♠	♥
171	«	↔	♠
172	¬	←	①
173	-	↑	②
174	®	→	③
175	¯	↓	④
176	°	°	⑤
177	±	±	⑥
178	²	″	⑦
179	³	≥	⑧
180	´	×	⑨
181	µ	∝	⑩
182	¶	∂	❶
183	·	•	❷
184	¸	÷	❸
185	¹	≠	❹
186	º	≡	❺
187	»	≈	❻
188	¼	…	❼

ANSI Code	Times	Symbol	Zapf Dingbats
189	½	│	❽
190	¾	—	❾
191	¿	↵	❿
192	À	ℵ	①
193	Á	ℑ	②
194	Â	ℜ	③
195	Ã	℘	④
196	Ä	⊗	⑤
197	Å	⊕	⑥
198	Æ	∅	⑦
199	Ç	∩	⑧
200	È	∪	⑨
201	É	⊃	⑩
202	Ê	⊇	❶
203	Ë	⊄	❷
204	Ì	⊂	❸
205	Í	⊆	❹
206	Î	∈	❺
207	Ï	∉	❻
208	Ð	∠	❼
209	Ñ	∇	❽
210	Ò	®	❾
211	Ó	©	❿
212	Ô	™	→
213	Õ	Π	→
214	Ö	√	↔
215	×	·	↕
216	Ø	¬	↘
217	Ù	∧	➡
218	Ú	∨	➚
219	Û	⇔	➔
220	Ü	⇐	➡
221	Ý	⇑	→
222	Þ	⇒	→

ANSI Code	Times	Symbol	Zapf Dingbats
223	ß	⇓	→
224	à	◊	⇒
225	á	〈	➡
226	â	®	➢
227	ã	©	➣
228	ä	™	➤
229	å	Σ	➥
230	æ	(	➦
231	ç	|	➧
232	è	\	➨
233	é	⌈	⇨
234	ê	|	⇨
235	ë	⌊	⇦
236	ì	(	⇦
237	í	⟨	⇨
238	î	⎩	⇨
239	ï	|	⇨
240	ð		
241	ñ	〉	⇨
242	ò	∫	↻
243	ó	⌠	➭
244	ô	|	➮
245	õ	⌡	➯
246	ö	)	➱
247	÷	|	➲
248	ø	)	➳
249	ù	⌉	➴
250	ú	|	➵
251	û	⌋	➶
252	ü	)	➷
253	ý	}	➸
254	þ	)	⇛
255	ÿ		

Ten Best-Kept Secrets

Every company has one of them—someone who just seems to know the coolest shortcuts in every program. You, too, can be one of those people. After you've mastered the top 10 tips in the Introduction, it's time to take a whack at QuarkXPress's best-kept secrets, the ones that make everyone gasp and mutter, "I didn't know you could do that!" You might already know some of these, but I bet one or two of them will be the jewel that gets you that raise you've been looking for.

1. **Spacebar at Launch**

   The XTensions Manager (Utilities→XTensions Manager) lets you turn on and off XTensions, but you have to relaunch the program to make the change take effect. Instead, try this. Quit XPress and then relaunch it. As soon as the program starts launching, hold down the spacebar and keep it held down until you see the XTensions Manager dialog box. If the program starts up without showing you the dialog box, you didn't hold down the spacebar early enough. Once the dialog box is visible, you can turn XTensions on and off and then let the program continue launching.

2. **Double-click for Tool Preferences**

   The more you customize QuarkXPress to the way you work, the more efficient you will be. For example, if you double-click on almost any tool in the Tool palette, XPress opens the Tool Preferences dialog box. From here, you can press the Modify button to change the way the tool works. I almost never make 1-point lines—most of my lines are .5-point thick—so I double-click on the Line tool, click Modify, and change the thickness to .5 pt. From now on, that tool will draw .5-point thick lines. Note that if you do this while no documents are open, it affects every new document you create from then on.

3. **Update Pictures with Subscriber Options**

   The Macintosh version of QuarkXPress has a feature in the Edit menu called Subscriber Options. Most people think this only works with the Macintosh operating system's Publish and Subscribe technology (which really sucks for professional publishing) so they ignore it. However, it also works with TIFF, JPEG, and EPS files! This comes in handy if you have dozens or hundreds of images in your document and you need to update one or two of them if, for example, they've been modified. The problem is that the more pictures you have in your document, the longer it takes for the Picture Usage dialog box to open. So, bypass Picture Usage entirely by opening Subscriber Options—the shortcut is to double-click on a picture box with the Content tool—and then press the Get Edition Now button. That updates just that one image.

4. Typing Absolute Page Numbers

Let's say you've used the Section feature (Page→Section) to start your document on a different page number, such as 47. Now you want to print the fifth page through the eighth page, but when you type 5 and 8 in the Print dialog box, you get an error that states there are no such pages. What do you do? Place a plus sign (+) before the numbers. Typing **+5** means the fifth page, no matter what page numbering scheme you're using.

5. Setting Tab Stops

Remember that when the Tab dialog box is open (Cmd+Shift+T or Ctrl+Shift+T), you can press Cmd+S or Ctrl+S to set a tab stop at whatever value you type in the Position field (it's the equivalent of clicking the Set button). Best of all, these shortcuts are great in conjunction with the math features. For example, if you want a tab stop every .6 inches, you can type **.6** and then Set, then **.6*2** then Set, then change **.6*3** then Set, and so on.

6. Changing Windows

When you have six document windows open at the same time and need to switch from one to the next, remember the Windows menu. On the PC, the Windows menu is obvious because it's at the top of the screen. However, on the Macintosh, you can Shift+click on the title bar of the topmost document to make the Window menu appear.

Note that the Window menu also offers Tile Documents and Stack Documents. When you hold down Option/Alt and select either of these, XPress automatically changes all the documents to Thumbnails view at the same time. This saves time when you have two documents open and you want to drag pages from one into the other.

On the other hand, if you are using QuarkXPress for Windows, you can type Ctrl+F6 and Ctrl+Shift+F6 to switch to the next or previous document window. I'm not sure why Quark hasn't included this in the Mac version.

7. **Converting Lines to Boxes**

   Draw a really thick line, set its style (such as arrowheads, dash, and so on), and then choose the Bézier box shape from the Item→Shape menu. (The Bézier box is the one that looks like a malformed kidney bean.) When you do this, XPress uses the outline of your line to define a new box. You can make some really cool effects with this.

8. **Closing Lines**

   Did you draw a Bézier line when you meant to draw a Bézier box? No problem. You know you can't just select the Bézier box from the Item→Shape menu (see previous tip). However, you *can* hold down the Option key when you select the Bézier box—this closes the two open ends of the path, turning the shape into a box.

9. **Text on a Circle**

   If you can draw a perfect circle with the Text on a Bézier Path tool, you're a better human than I. That's okay because I've got a trick to get text on a circle. Draw a circular text box (remember to hold down the Shift key to constrain the shape to a circle, unless you want an oval) and then put text inside it. Now, select the Bézier line shape from the Item→Shape menu—that's the one that looks like a squiggle. Voilà! The text now follows the circular shape. One last step: Set the color of the path to None, or you'll see the circle under the text.

10. **Deselect All**

    One of my favorites, perhaps because I talked the Quark product manager into including this shortcut, is this: Press the Tab key when you have the Item tool selected, and the program automatically deselects everything on the page. It also works when you have two or more objects selected with the Content tool.

Index

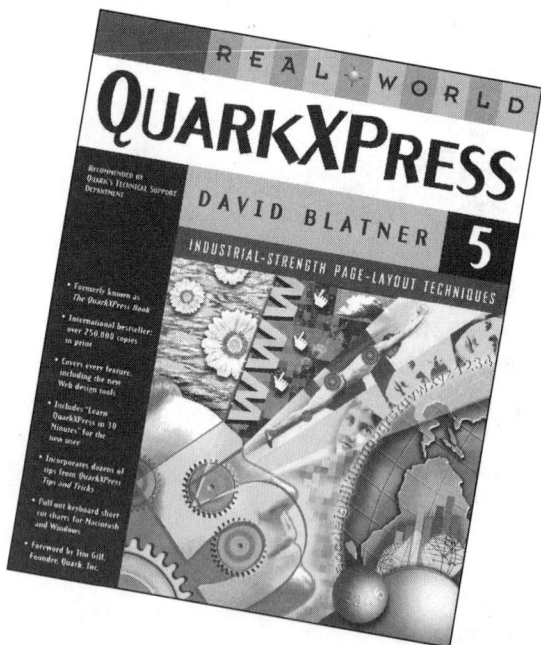